Invented Voices

BOOKS BY DONALD NEWLOVE

NOVELS

The Painter Gabriel

Sweet Adversity
embodying the author's final revisions of his
Siamese twin novels,
Leo & Theodore and *The Drunks*

Eternal Life

Curranne Trueheart

Starlite Photoplays
a trilogy embodying the completed and forthcoming

Marlon and Meryl Together at Last:
A Village Romance

Buckangel:
A Screwball Tragedy Starring Cary Grant

The Welles Requiem

ON WRITING

Those Drinking Days:
Myself and Other Writers

First Paragraphs:
Inspired Openings for Writers and Readers

Painted Paragraphs:
Inspired Description for Writers and Readers

Invented Voices:
Inspired Dialogue for Writers and Readers

A HANDBOOK FOR THE SOUL

Invented Voices

INSPIRED DIALOGUE FOR
WRITERS AND READERS

DONALD NEWLOVE

HENRY HOLT AND COMPANY NEW YORK

Henry Holt and Company, Inc.
Publishers since 1866
115 West 18th Street
New York, New York 10011

Henry Holt® is a registered
trademark of Henry Holt and Company, Inc.

Published in Canada by Fitzhenry & Whiteside Ltd.,
195 Allstate Parkway, Markham, Ontario L3R 4T8.

Library of Congress Cataloging-in-Publication Data
Newlove, Donald.
Invented voices: inspired dialogue for writers and readers /
Donald Newlove.
p.   cm.
At head of title: A handbook for the soul.
Includes index.
1. Literature—Collections.   2. Dialogues.   I. Title.   II. Title:
Handbook for the soul.
PN6014.N47   1994
808.8'026—dc20   94-1565
                                                              CIP

ISBN 0-8050-2979-6

Henry Holt books are available for special
promotions and premiums. For details contact:
Director, Special Markets.

First Edition—1994

DESIGNED BY PAULA R. SZAFRANSKI

Printed in the United States of America
All first editions are printed on acid-free paper.∞
1   3   5   7   9   10   8   6   4   2

For LISA,
whose eyes hold
the colors of the rain
and whose laugh
holds life

Letter to the Reader

This rounds out my three book-length essays on what makes writing breathe.

Nowhere do I tell you how to sell your work—or even how to write it. Begun with *First Paragraphs: Inspired Openings for Writers and Readers* and carried on with *Painted Paragraphs: Inspired Description for Writers and Readers,* this trilogy strives only to bring fresh air to your furnace and brighten the coals. These are handbooks for the soul.

Few people grasp just how deeply writers write for themselves before their writing passes into printer's ink and becomes a public act. For sheer privacy poets are even worse. Rainer Maria Rilke couldn't care less if you read his poems. You are the farthest thing from his mind as he unleaves his core and imprints his findings into a phrase on paper. "Who, if I called out, would hear me among the angelic orders?" he asks. He's writing for angels. Great dialogue springs from privacy, a place where all is fresh and yearning and the heart unbound by any commerce but with itself. The most private writer ever—and yet today the most public—is Wild Bill Shakespeare, the bulk of whose writing is dialogue.

This book brims over with stage, movie, and television dialogue, a rigorously public kind of writing. Much of the most exciting dialogue of the century is written for movies, though as you'll see, we finally do slip from under the arms of filmmaking, and the art of rewriting novel dialogue for the screen, and get into print dialogue.

You may be reading this to brush up on writing salable, public dialogue. Fine. Everything in this book was written for the public and sold. But I warn you now, *great* dialogue—dialogue that replenishes the spirit—is between the self and the soul. Not you and the bank.

There's a hazy figure given out by Hollywood screenwriters that some two thousand scripts get written for each one produced—which may or may not include rewrites by additional writers. Over the years, I've rewritten for film a number of my own published works, sometimes with screen options, sometimes not, but none has finally made it to film. Writing movies is fun, a big juggling act with all balls floating in the air at once, and nothing can take from my joy at having written lines that satisfy my thirst to write for voice, not just print.

All dialogue starts as a fearless big valve of a voice alone in the shower. Movie dialogue, once it becomes a public act, touches us because it speaks to us privately, even in a crowd, and awakens us to something common but freshly seen or heard in the writer's heart. He may tell us that to a mass murderer life's but a walking shadow or brief candle, a tale told by an idiot, full of sound and fury, signifying nothing, and we know at once that beyond the public import of these metaphors lies a personal peril the writer has taken with himself, a darkness he has walked into or found under his own skin—in this case Shakespeare's skin. Dramatic dialogue gathers power when a writer looks at the poor, bare, forked animal he is and tells us what he sees, through the masks of his characters as one after another he slips into them.

But as soon as the writer writes directly for the public, he cheats. First he cheats himself, by dealing in secondhand feelings, stale rages, and prosy fist-wavings, and he cheats the public, giving it dead fruit freshly waxed. Private, original work springs from the unconscious and demands a new framework or plot, something never before seen and which may go long unvalued because of its newness. Nor is emotional logic in drama a problem of craft. If you have no fresh perils to report from your unconscious, you have no play and must fall back on craft and the tried and true: sex, suspense, hardware, consumer fantasies, folksiness, or whatever.

A wordless urgency brings us the voices most apt to embody our joy in being able to grasp another human being and shape his or her spirit in dialogue. The art lies in letting characters speak in their own voices and not as puppets. In *Richard III*, in one of Shakespeare's greatest scenes (act 1, scene 4), two stony-eyed murderers come to the Tower of London to kill the prisoner Clarence but fall into moral hairsplitting and fits of conscience, then even confer with their victim about the justice of their act. The Second Murderer at last says, "Look behind you, my lord," upon which the First Murderer stabs Clarence, crying, "Take that, and that; if all this will not do, I'll drown you in the malmsey-butt within." And as the First Murderer drowns the bleeding Clarence in a vat of wine, the Second Murderer's remorse returns and he chooses to skip payment for their deed. Shakespeare puts his ear to a murderer's spirit and catches the horror with perfect pitch. One reaches back through time into that stillness in which Wild Bill sat listening to his quarreling murderers and questioning victim, and it's like pressing your own ear to a room full of mutterings in which Shakespeare the victim sits splitting moral laws about his own murder with Shakespeare the double-minded villain. *I'm about to be murdered by these idiots!*

Such urgent thoughts between you and your soul can be written only in a very private place.

—Donald Newlove

Invented Voices

All dialogue is between the self and the soul.

Whether Tolstoy or Shakespeare, or a skit writer for "Roseanne" as she mashes her family into a ball, you *are* all your characters. They spring from you and each demands you stand up for him or against the others. All their problems turn into moral problems as you enact judgment.

In this book we watch writers allow characters to grow through dialogue about moral action.

Dialogue differs in the novel, short story, movie, opera, stage play, sitcom, radio play, cartoon, or any other form. Each form thrives on its own echo of human speech. People in novels never speak like people in sitcoms or with the big feelings of opera folk. Each form makes its own contract with the audience. We must square within ourselves what our characters say to the larger audience and ask ourselves tirelessly, Do I *mean* this? If we cheat on the moral hunger of our characters, and go for the laugh or zinger, we lose spirit and soon mutter, "Cheap shot, cheap shot." Memorable dialogue replenishes us, though dull readers often choose books by their white space—lots of talk, hey, an easy read. Junk food goes down easy, too. Hell, movie scripts scream for More White Space. This very book boasts tons of attractive white space. But with memorable dialogue, we savor each word, however light the page, and drink from the soul.

The only law of dialogue: it must entertain. You can say anything—*anything*—as long as you say it entertainingly and appeal to the reader's or viewer's sense of play. Play implies imagination—and we go to our graves still ravenous for stories. Playfulness is the first quality of genius—without it we're earthbound. Somebody wants to write a creation myth, he makes up the character God, whose first line is "Let there be light." This entertains us deeply. A child or a hundred-year-old man grasps it at once—the child with even livelier imagination. And yet one of the deepest mysteries binding men together—the birth of light—reaches us in exalted language that speaks forcefully in all tongues—just because it caresses and entertains our deepest being. The glory and fall of Adam and Eve—the first story taught to children at Sunday school—sounds our depths with sin, innocence, sex, and Paradise—the core of our being. What could be richer storytelling? We plumb this story tirelessly all our lives. Disobedience of divine law requires daily that even the atheist weigh himself as good or evil, for he too must answer "Does evil exist and does it exist in me?" This poetic tale that some scholar of Judean folk wisdom wrote remains the fulcrum of our spiritual balance. Why? We can never solve its immense mystery—and mysteries entertain.

In whatever format, all dialogue is artificial—even God's. At times actors improvise and achieve a staged illogic that sounds real—but all mimicry of human thought is artificial. In adapting middleweight champion Jake La Motta's life story for Martin Scorsese's strongest work, *Raging Bull* (1980), scripters Paul Schrader and Mardik Martin provide lines that become dancing springboards for actors Robert De Niro (as Jake) and Joe Pesci (as Jake's trainer and brother, Joey La Motta). My favorite scene explodes in Jake's grungy living room as he tries to shake a picture into his early-model television set. Joey lies on the couch. The shooting script has these lines:

JOEY

You're worried about this girl, you're gonna let this girl ruin your life for you . . . You wanna worry, worry about your stomach that you can't bend over—that you gotta step into the ring in a month.

JAKE

Did you ever fuck my wife?

JOEY

What?

JAKE

I don't mean now. I mean *before*—before we met.

JOEY

Whadda ya mean?

JAKE

Did you ever fuck my wife?

JOEY

Whatsa matter with you?

JAKE

You're very smart, Joey, very smart. Nobody gives me a straight answer around here. You're givin' me these answers, but you still didn't answer my question. Did you fuck Vickie?

JOEY
(fed up, he starts to leave)
I gotta go. I gotta get outta here. I can't take this shit. Lenore is waitin' for me. I gotta go. You're fuckin' crazy, you know that, crazy.

JOEY leaves.

The lines give no hint of De Niro's soft-spoken restraint as he reads them, nor of Joey's poker face, which hints of lying—though he says nothing dishonest. Is Jake paranoid? we wonder. Actually, Joey hides the fact that Vickie might have bedded a handsome hood whom Joey beat up when he flirted with Vickie in the Copacabana nitery.

The lines in the finished film:

JOEY

You meathead, you're lettin' this girl ruin your life, lookit choo. She really did some job on you. You know how fuckin' nuts you are? Look what she did to you.

JAKE

You fucked my wife?

JOEY

What!?

JAKE

You fucked my wife?

How could you ask me a question like that? How could
you ask me, I'm your brother. You asked me that?
Where do you get your balls big enough to ask *me* that?

JAKE

Just tell me.

JOEY

I'm not answering you. I can't answer that, it's stupid.

JAKE

You're very smart, Joey. You're givin' me all these
answers but you ain't givin' me the right answer. I'll ask
you again. Did you or did you not?

JOEY

I'm not gonna answer. That's a sick question, you're a
sick fuck, but I'm not that sick that I'm gonna answer it.
I'm not tellin' you anything. I'm gonna leave. So Lenore
calls, tell her I went home. I'm not stayin' in this nut
house with you. You're a sick bas— I feel sorry for you, I
really do. You know what you should do? Try a little
more fuckin' and a little less eatin' and you won't have
troubles upstairs in your bedroom and you won't take it
out on me and everybody else. Understand, you fuckin'
wacko? You're crackin' up. Fuckin' screwball you.

JOEY leaves.

The improvised lines boost the scene mightily and let the
actors dig into feelings the writers don't explore as deeply.
De Niro plays superbly throughout, just about whispering.
He wants to know and he doesn't want to, and his voice
strikes a pleading note we first heard in Marlon Brando's
failed prizefighter in *On the Waterfront* (1954)—a film
quoted at length in *Raging Bull* by fat and aging Jake La

Motta as a bar shill in Florida who imitates Brando for a stage act.

So what *is* the writers' role in this scene? First, they give it structure. Whoever plays it, they built it. Pianists say of Beethoven's late sonatas that he writes better than anyone can play. When I first read Shakespeare I thought the depths of his poetry lay far beyond actors. We don't think that about a shooting script. These lines lie within the compass of any gifted actor—no long tradition hallows them. And yet when De Niro and Pesci read them, after many, many freewheeling rehearsals, and when after many viewings we see at last how carefully and with what patience De Niro lovingly carries Pesci through the scene, feeding him opening after emotional opening, almost begging him, in a whisper, to hurt him, tell him that he fucked Vickie, he just wants the truth, we know that the lines could not possibly have been read better by Brando himself or any other two actors. For me, Jake's turning against everyone who supports him—now that he has at last won the title—becomes the picture's pivotal and richest scene. He's not worthy of this honor or them and must bring his house down on his head. Smash Joey, smash Vickie, and out of some rocklike sense of honor smash his title.

But what if the scene had been played as written? For an answer, let's look to Brando's pug in the Budd Schulberg script for Elia Kazan's *On the Waterfront*. Charley "The Gent" Malloy (Rod Steiger), once his brother Terry's manager in the ring, now runs with the waterfront union hoods while lightly punch-drunk and puffy-lidded Terry (Brando) spits his life away working the docks. One night in a taxi, Charley warns Terry not to sing to the Crime Commission about a union-led murder he unwittingly took part in.

Charley pulls a gun on his brother, who guides it aside. Schulberg's shooting script gives them these lines:

TERRY
(an accusing sigh)
Wow. . . .

CHARLEY
(gently)
What do you weigh these days, slugger?

TERRY
(shrugs)
—eighty-seven, eighty-eight. What's it to you?

CHARLEY
(nostalgically)
Gee, when you tipped one seventy-five, you were beautiful. You should've been another Billy Conn. That skunk I got to manage you brought you along too fast.

TERRY
It wasn't him!
(years of abuse crying out in him)
It was you, Charley. You and Johnny. Like the night the two of youse come in the dressing room and says, 'Kid, this ain't your night—we're going for the price on Wilson.' *It ain't my night.* I'd of taken Wilson apart that night! I was ready—remember the early rounds throwing them combinations. So what happens—This bum Wilson he gets the title shot—outdoors in the ball park!—and what do I get—a couple of bucks and a one-way ticket to Palookaville. *(more and more aroused as he relives it)* It was you, Charley. You was my brother. You should of looked out for me. Instead of making me take them dives for the short-end money.

CHARLEY
(defensively)
I always had a bet down for you. You saw some money.

TERRY
(agonized)
See! You don't understand!

CHARLEY
I tried to keep you in good with Johnny.

TERRY
You don't understand! I could've been a contender. I could've had class and been somebody. Real class. Instead of a bum, let's face it, which is what I am. It was you, Charley.

But the actors, swept up by their feelings, read the lines this way:

TERRY
(turning gun away)
Charley. . . . Ah, Charley. . . . Wow.

CHARLEY
Look, kid. . . . How much you weigh, son? When you weighed one hundred and sixty-eight pounds, you were beautiful. Youda been another Billy Conn. But that skunk we got ya for a manager, we brought you along too fast.

TERRY
It wasn't him, Charley, it was *you*. Remember that night in the garden, you came down to my dressing room and said, 'Kid, this ain't your night. We're goin' for the price on Wilson.' Ya remember that? *This ain't your night*—my night!? I coulda taken Wilson apart. And what happens, he gets the title shot outdoors in the ball park and what

8

am I gettin'?—a one-way ticket to Palookaville. You was my brother, Charley, you shoulda looked out for me a little bit. You shoulda taken care of me just a little bit so I wouldn't have to take them dives for the short-end money.

CHARLEY

I had some bets down for ya. You saw some money.

TERRY

You don't understand! I coulda had class! I coulda been a contender! I coulda *been* somebody. Instead of a bum, which is what I am, let's face it. It was you, Charley.

Some phrases drop away, others run together, and a much greater intensity arises on Schulberg's structure. Brando makes a slight gaff, saying that he had to take more than the one dive that Schulberg focuses on with Wilson. We see Terry somewhat differently when he's trapped into "them dives" for the short-end money *after* the fall with Wilson.

Schulberg slaved over his dialogue and spent a year on the docks taking down dockworkers' talk. But he tells us in *On the Waterfront: A Screenplay* (Southern Illinois University Press, 1980):

At the outset Gadg (Kazan) had made his promise not to change a line of the script, but I would have to make a counter-promise: either to be on the set with him every day or to be on call to make the changes accommodating the practical and creative exigencies. . . . Gadg kept his promise. Oh sure, lines overlapped, good, fresh words were thrown in spontaneously, but scene by scene Gadg stuck to the script, inventing and improving with staging that surprised and delighted me.

This scene—the moral climax, and the last footage shot for the picture—ends the second act. The third act bursts with action. The money'd run out and only the backseat of a cab could be afforded for a set, with the least costly lighting setup and a strange venetian blind over the cab's back window so that rear projection of the streets could be avoided. In a sweat like that, and with Steiger and Brando ("Wow-w") breathing each word with sublime self-confidence (though Steiger's rising tears ruined many takes), what writer would carp that his lines got mangled—or in fact improved?

Is dialogue stronger in *Raging Bull* or *Waterfront*? Both Scorsese and Kazan want living blood pumping out of the screen. In both cases art demands artifice—much gets trimmed in order to arrive at the structure in each passage so that the actors' intensity need not waver through the pointless stammerings and jabber of normal talk. Each scene feeds on a spine, or through-line, that keeps the actors focused and powerful. No matter what the actors improvise, the scene can never be rehearsed or played exactly the same twice—feelings will always subtly shift the sense. Moreover, both scenes—the emotional heart of each film—must deliver. Although the lines in "Did you fuck my wife?" don't seem to carry this weight, the ones in "I coulda been a contender" do, especially when Schulberg's stage directions tell us, "years of abuse crying out in him" and "agonized." Each scene ends the second act, with a half-hour's playing time left in each film. The third acts will only mop up the action and never again hit the emotional peak of the fat second acts, the breadbaskets of their dramas. We might think that Jake beating his head on the wall of his jail cell ends *Raging Bull* with even greater intensity—but no wisdom comes from his suffering. For me the most intense moment—his split with Joey—propels Jake into the third act.

I'd say "Did you fuck my wife?" asks more understanding from us than the agony of "I coulda been a contender," though De Niro as straight man to Pesci plays with matchless richness and restraint—"Just tell me, Joey, did you or did you not?"—as does Brando with Steiger—"It was you, Charley"—each actor inviting us with a voice soft as feathers into his character's inmost agony.

Nothing underlines the scene's importance to Jake, the lines breeze by. Everyone involved must have talked and talked it out. As soon as Joey leaves, Jake feels overwhelmed by Vickie's betrayal—or his self-betrayal seen in her. For her he took a crushing, heartbreaking dive so that later he could get a title shot, the belt, and be a king in her eyes as well as his own. But now as champ, he feels even more sure that she's fucking behind his back. "I don't trust anything about her," he tells Joey, who knows that Jake's a fruitcake, no longer trusting anyone, or anything about himself, and burying himself in food.

Did the scenes as written have power? Of course. But the directors and actors enriched them. Film writers have unions and try for contractual guarantees to protect their lines. When director Mike Nichols filmed Edward Albee's play *Who's Afraid of Virginia Woolf?* (from a script by Ernest Lehman), there was no room for actors and director to improvise—not that some scenes don't move outdoors and, at a roadhouse, add a few trivial new lines by Lehman. The whole show lay in film actors ripping into already-famous stage lines, with Richard Burton—a stage professional—underplaying his lines and not giving the stronger reading he had in him. Improvising and knocking the lines around to get more richly into his character might have freed him when he went back to his usual line-perfect reading. As for the writers on these three movies, their goal of actually getting a strong story on film calls for give-and-take, with the money peaches and cream—though I know Albee wondered what foreign language his characters had fallen into with Lehman's lines. No one—*no one*—can write lines for your characters that don't ring false to you.

The pivotal dialogue in Joseph Heller's satiric novel *Catch-22* (and in Mike Nichols's movie version) comes about a tenth of the way into the story. Captain Yossarian, a U.S. bomber pilot stationed on the Mediterranean island of Pianosa during World War II, sees flak lay open his bombardier's guts during a mission and now wants to have himself declared crazy and grounded as unfit for combat. He goes to see Doc Daneeka:

"You're wasting your time," Doc Daneeka was forced to tell him.

"Can't you ground someone who's crazy?"

"Oh, sure. I have to. There's a rule saying I have to ground anyone who's crazy."

"Then why don't you ground me? I'm crazy. Ask Clevinger." [Clevinger's sure Yossarian's crazy.]

"Clevinger? Where is Clevinger? You find Clevinger and I'll ask him."

"Then ask any of the others. They'll tell you how crazy I am."

"They're crazy."

"Then why don't you ground them?"

"Why don't they ask me to ground them?"

"Because they're crazy, that's why."

"Of course they're crazy," Doc Daneeka replied. "I just told you they're crazy, didn't I? And you can't let crazy people decide whether you're crazy or not, can you?"

Yossarian looked at him soberly and tried another approach. "Is Orr crazy?"

"He sure is," Doc Daneeka said.

"Can you ground him?"

"I sure can. But first he has to ask me to. That's part of the rule."

"Then why doesn't he ask you to?"

"Because he's crazy," Doc Daneeka said. "He has to be crazy to keep flying combat missions after all the close calls he's had. Sure, I can ground Orr. But first he has to ask me to."

"That's all it takes to be grounded?"

"That's all. Let him ask me."

"And then you can ground him," Yossarian asked.

"No. Then I can't ground him."

"You mean there's a catch?"

"Sure there's a catch," Doc Daneeka replied. "Catch-22. Anyone who wants to get out of combat duty isn't really crazy."

There was only one catch and that was Catch-22, which specified that a concern for one's own safety in the face of dangers that were real and immediate was the process of a rational mind. Orr was crazy and could be grounded. All he had to do was ask; and as soon as he did, he would no longer be crazy and would have to fly more missions. Orr would be crazy to fly more missions and sane if he didn't, but if he was sane he had to fly them. If he flew them he was crazy and didn't have to; but if he didn't want to he was sane and had to. Yossarian was moved very deeply by the absolute simplicity of this clause of Catch-22 and let out a respectful whistle.

"That's some catch, that Catch-22," he observed.

"It's the best there is," Doc Daneeka agreed.

—*Catch-22* (1961),
Joseph Heller

Buck Henry's script of this scene for Mike Nichols's unfairly bashed film of *Catch-22* follows Heller quite closely, cuts the talk by a third, and ends it with topsy-turvy brilliance by having Yossarian (Alan Arkin) hanging upside down from the nose hatch of his moving bomber, crying, "That's some catch, that Catch-22!" while Doc Daneeka (Jack Gilford) runs upside down from Yossarian's point of view, shouting into Yossarian's face, "It's the best there is!" Novelist–film critic David Thomson—whose *Biographical Dictionary of Film* packs rich, enlivening thoughts into small spaces, sometimes at the cost of sense—calls Nichols's film an "intrinsically cold, great technical achievement" that "did not derive from a felt experience of Americana so much as a mocking intellectual critique of it." It watched pain without itself suffering, he went on. Since I suffered nothing in reading the novel, laughed only in fits and starts, and found its second half bookishly black, I didn't expect felt experience and suffering in the movie. Thomson mistakes Yossarian's life-hungry, long-faced, lizard-eyed view of death in battle, the core feeling enacted both in novel and film, for Nichols's unfelt, cold expertise. The film pleased Heller—who said after a preview, "It's the greatest movie I've ever seen!"—and should live long after its middling reviews fade. The movie's later descent into darkness follows the dark last third of the novel, by which time Heller's humor loses heart and overstays itself by a hundred pages. More so than the published version, the impressionistic, Joycean original manuscript, typed nearly wall-to-wall on over eight hundred pages, laid on a much darker mock-formlessness whose meticulous structure, Heller says, made clear his view of the absurdity of war. But he chose to go with a cut version, with its loony Marx Brothers dialogue fading into a much shorter dark night than he first drew, and I respect his lightening the gloom. Heavy trimming may give questionable pages space to breathe. If you can't decide, *cut*—no one will miss it, even you after your feelings shake down, and the reader may well bless your swift mind. Had Heller cut even more than the 175 pages he did cut (he saved all the story turns and cut much cuckoobird dialogue), he might have a bouncier, less grand work that demands less of the reader but betrays the novel's vision. So, is *Catch-22* merely an overweight novel that strives for mightiness but loses its comic spirit— or is it a thorough success, with the comic spirit only part of a larger strategy? This question broaches its own artistic Catch-22, since most readers find themselves drawn to the book for its humor and don't expect to wind up in Dostoyevsky and Céline, where Heller takes them. Well, the novel's grand design succeeds with Heller and laggers behind will simply have to catch up.

How does the Doc Daneeka passage work? Out of twenty-five mostly brief exchanges, only nine name the speaker, which lends fleetness. I suspect that this patch of dialogue once went on a bit longer and has been smartly abridged, with the prose paragraph that now caps it spelling out the theme. He wants his big theme made clear in his own voice and not simply enacted in dialogue. There's no drawing of faces, no fluttering eyebrow writing, no hint of tones of voice. HEARING THESE LINES OVER THE ROAR OF A BOMBER ABOUT TO TAKE OFF, AS IN THE FILM, ADDS WONDERFULLY TO THEIR FORCE!! The final two-line tag drives home the insanity of the novel's guiding vision of war—*and* of the postwar era Heller lived through during his four years of writing *Catch-22* in the late fifties. The loco universe of *Catch-22* imprisons us during peace as well as war. Ideal readers no longer come to it with the same single-minded thirst for lunacy with which I came thirty years ago.

I enjoy setting key passages of dialogue from novels beside their reworkings as screenplays, one of my favorites being that where Casper Gutman lets Sam Spade in on the secret of the Maltese falcon. Dashiell Hammett's *The Maltese Falcon* (1929) has been filmed three times, but only once with art. The first version, called *The Maltese Falcon* (1931) but for television later retitled *Dangerous Female*, follows rather closely this famous scene as it appears in the novel but tries to boost Sam Spade's suavity. Roy Del Ruth directs fast but uninspiredly, with Ricardo Cortez as Spade to Dudley Digges's Gutman. Version two, William Dieterle's busy but empty *Satan Met a Lady* (1936), replaces the falcon with the Horn of Roland, gives Gutman's great speeches to comic actor Arthur Treacher, and recasts Gutman as a woman. It's a mess, but lecherous Warren William as Ted Shayne (Spade) blithely feels up both Marie Wilson, his secretary, and Bette Davis, the lying murderess. We'll follow John Huston's dialogue for his *The Maltese Falcon* (1941), the talkiest version of the three but a supreme script only Shakespeare could improve—Spade cribs the last line, not in the novel, from *The Tempest*.

One afternoon Huston—called away to work on another picture—told his secretary to type up all the dialogue in Hammett's novel in script format. This became *the* script. He tells us in his autobiography (*An Open Book*, 1980): "During the entire filming not one line of dialogue was changed. One short scene was dropped when I realized I could substitute a telephone call for it without loss to the story." Of how many adaptations can this be said!

In the novel Gutman unloads far more text on Spade than this scene can handle on film and Huston cuts it in half. A marvelously fat, sleek, shiny-eyed smiling villain, Sydney Greenstreet, made even fatter with a pillow, plays Gutman to Humphrey Bogart's hardboiled Sam Spade:

GUTMAN

By gad, sir, you're a chap worth knowing. An amazing character. Gimme your hat. Sit down there. I owe you an apology, sir.

SPADE

Never mind that. Let's talk about the black bird.

GUTMAN

All right, sir, let's. Let's. This is going to be the most astounding thing you've ever heard of, sir, and I say this, knowing that a man of your calibre and your profession must have known some astounding things in his time. What do you know, sir, about the Order of the Hospital of Saint John of Jerusalem, later known as the Knights of Rhodes and other things?

SPADE

Crusaders or something, weren't they?

GUTMAN

Very good. Sit down. In 1539, these Crusading Knights persuaded Emperor Charles the Fifth to give them the Island of Malta. He made but one condition. That they pay him each year the tribute of a falcon in acknowledgement that Malta was still under Spain. Do you follow me?

SPADE

Uh-huh.

GUTMAN

Have you any conception of the extreme, the immeasurable wealth of the Order at that time?

SPADE

I imagine they were pretty well fixed.

GUTMAN

Pretty well is putting it mildly. They were rolling in wealth, sir. For years they'd taken from the East, nobody knows what spoils of gems, precious metals, silks, ivory, sir. We all know that the Holy Wars to them were largely a matter of loot. The Knights were profoundly grateful to the Emperor Charles for his generosity toward them. They hit upon the happy thought of sending him for his first year's tribute not an insignificant live bird but a glorious golden falcon crusted from head to foot with the finest jewels in their coffers. Well, sir—what do you think?

SPADE

I don't know.

GUTMAN

These are facts, historical facts; not school book history, not Mr. Wells' history, but history, nevertheless. They sent this foot-high jeweled bird to Charles who was then in Spain. They sent it in a galley commanded by a member of the Order. It never reached Spain. A famous admiral of buccaneers took the Knights' galley and the bird. In 1713 it turned up in Sicily. In 1840 it appeared in Paris. It had, by that time, acquired a coat of black enamel so that it looked nothing more than a fairly interesting black statuette. In that disguise, sir, it was as you may say, kicked around Paris for over three score years by private owners too stupid to see what it was under the skin. Then h'mm, in 1923 a Greek dealer named Charilaos Konstantinides found it in an obscure shop. No thickness of enamel could conceal value from his eyes. You begin to believe me a little?

SPADE

Haven't said I didn't.

GUTMAN

Well, sir, to hold it safe while pursuing his researches into its history, Charilaos re-enamelled the bird. Despite this precaution, however, I got wind of his find. Ah, if I'd only known a few days sooner. I was in London when I heard. I packed a bag, got on the boat train immediately. On the train I opened the paper, the *Times*, and read that Charilaos's establishment had been burglarized and him murdered. Sure enough, on arriving there I discovered the bird was gone. That was seventeen years ago. Well, sir, it took me seventeen years to locate the bird, but I did. I wanted it! I'm a man not easily discouraged when I want something. I traced it to the home of a Russian general—one Kemidov, in an Istanbul suburb. He didn't know a thing about it. It was nothing but a black enamelled figure to him, but his natural contrariness kept him from selling it to me but I made him an offer. So I sent him some, er, agents to get it. Well, sir, they got it and I haven't got it, but I'm going to get it. Your glass.

SPADE

Well, then, the bird doesn't really belong to any of you, but to a General Kemidov?

GUTMAN

Well sir, you might as well say it belonged to the King of Spain. I don't see how you can honestly grant anyone else a clear title to it, except by right of possession.

—*The Maltese Falcon* (1941),
script by John Huston,
from the book by Dashiell Hammett (1929)

Spade plays straight man while the fat clown Gutman dishes up the falcon's history, each historical fact long-pickled and toothsome. Greenstreet turns these lines into an actor's feast. As the imaginative heart of the black comedy, with Spade soon felled by drugged whiskey, Gutman's monologue climaxes the second act. Once more, the third act tidies up the action. But the glow of Greenstreet's reading of the history of the black bird casts glory over the whole film.

Where did this speech come from? Hammett says he read about a rental agreement between Charles V and the Knights Hospitaler, and about the tribute of a live falcon, and it all stuck with him, though he imagined the bejeweled falcon. However, a retired detective and ex-partner of Hammett's, Phil Haultain, told Hammett biographer William F. Nolan that the falcon sprang from a jeweled skull from Calcutta. The object—taken as loot by a member of the British Expedition to India—had a gory history, being the skull of a holy man from Lhasa, Tibet. Haultain's uncle sent it to Haultain and the ex-partner showed it to Hammett, whose memory folded it in with falcon. Did Hammett invent first a fake bejeweled skull, and only as an inspired afterthought marry it to the live falcon remade as an encrusted statuette, as Haultain suggests? We'll never know. But that so-called bejeweled skull sounds like a gewgaw that can't match the original falcon's worth.

The falcon and the skull become one in Hammett's mind as a focus for his theme, the illusions of greed. Gutman thinks he first found the falcon seventeen years before. But when unwrapped at the story's end, Gutman's falcon proves a lead knockoff. All of the criminals around Gutman believe so strongly in his having once sighted the real black bird that they kill to own it. But as Spade's curtain line puts it, this bird's only "the stuff that dreams are made of." Still, Gutman wishes to spend one more year chasing after Kemidov and the bird in Istanbul. Bogart himself suggested to Huston the turn on "We are such stuff as dreams are made of" while filming the last scene, which lacked a punchy exit line. Otherwise, Dashiell Hammett wrote the script, albeit unwittingly, adapting his novel with rare honesty. When studio head Jack Warner happened on the secretary's typed-up dialogue, his delight over "Huston's" work bloomed. "It's a great script!"

Within the next ten years Huston's films drew from two more novels about greed and illusion, B. Traven's *The Treasure of the Sierra Madre* (1948) and W. R. Burnett's *The Asphalt Jungle* (1950). In the scene below, Huston and fellow screenwriter Ben Maddow compose a pivotal scene while scripting *The Asphalt Jungle*. Burnett, famed for his crime classics *Little Caesar* and *High Sierra*, liked all the script but the last scene and thought the finished film the best crime movie ever made. Though not pivotal in the novel, the scene we'll read sets up the end of the second act and crooked lawyer Alonzo P. Emmerich's suicide, and at the same time it eloquently spells out the theme. Once more, the third act is all action.

Huston seeks two lines of storytelling in *Jungle*. First he shows thieves plotting the Midwest's biggest jewel heist ever, and blueprints for us what goes into pulling this off: getting the cash to plan with; hiring a safecracker at ease with nitro, a hoodlum for firearms, and a getaway man; and then fencing the take. "The Professor" (Sam Jaffe) who masterminds the heist says of the hoods under him, "They'll not be told about the size of the take. Sometimes men get greedy." Each character has his human side, his goals, his vice. Huston and Maddow take as much care with this "non-action" human side as with the caper, showing us the safecracker's family, the love of horses in the armed lookout, the loyal comrade in the hunchbacked getaway driver. Though we admire The Professor's plan keenly, blind accident undermines its perfection. "Greed made me blind!" he says, lying wounded in bed. As for his satchel full of jewels: "As things stand, it's just so much junk."

The story turns also on the double-dealing of Emmerich (Louis Calhern), the shyster who attempts to run off with the loot. He tells a debt-collecting private detective he hires: "Bob—I'm broke! That's the plain, simple fact. Finished. Bankrupt. . . . It's true. I can't believe it myself, but it's true. Sure, I get big fees, but they're spent before they're collected. . . . Mortgaged—up to here. . . . Every time I turn around it costs thousands of dollars, ten thousand here, ten thousand there."

Emmerich tries to outfox the thieves, but they kill Bob the private detective bloodily in Emmerich's living room and Emmerich's world unravels beyond mere money and bankruptcy. Beside himself with tension, he goes upstairs to visit his sickly wife and sits calmly talking with her while dying inside.

INT. MRS. EMMERICH'S BEDROOM
Hearing Emmerich's step on the stair, she makes an involuntary gesture toward arranging her hair. Emmerich enters.

MRS. EMMERICH
Can we go on playing?

EMMERICH
All right.
He sits down on the bed. Her face shows concern.

MRS. EMMERICH

Why, you're as pale as a ghost. What's the matter?

EMMERICH

I heard some bad news. Man who was working for me got killed.

MRS. EMMERICH

Oh, Lon, how awful! Was it an accident?

EMMERICH
(shakes his head)

No. It was an intentional killing.

MRS. EMMERICH

What was his name?

EMMERICH

Brannom. He had a private detective agency.

MRS. EMMERICH

Do they know who did it?
(Emmerich shakes his head)

Lon, when I think about all those awful people you come in contact with—downright criminals—I get scared.

EMMERICH

There's nothing so different about them.
(Something in his tone strikes her as queer. Watching him, she frowns slightly.)
—After all, crime is only a left-handed form of human endeavor.

She is studying his face as we

DISSOLVE.

Where *The Maltese Falcon* blooms from Hammett's sense of language, with Hammett plotting only a half-page ahead of us as he writes, Burnett's novel builds on plot and incident, with mood and heightened language lesser concerns. Hammett builds toward the big speeches. Burnett, and then Maddow and Huston, want us to sense the jungle of a huge, sprawling Midwestern city (Chicago served for the shoot), and they have their speeches, but more intently they unearth a crime's dark roots and watch the law thrash lawbreakers out of shadows. Like Hammett, they light their story with an unwavering theme: the costs of the misuse of human intelligence. Says the police commissioner (John McIntire) about Emmerich: "Married twenty years, and consorting with a woman young enough to be his granddaughter [Marilyn Monroe]. It's disgusting.—But nothing could surprise me about Emmerich. An educated man who uses his brains to circumvent the law.—Worst type of human being. No excuse for him."

This really stretches us, an appraisal of Emmerich by an educated peer which nails him solidly and makes us sigh for our own sins as educated people. These words match Emmerich's own appraisal of his peers in crime: "After all, crime is only a left-handed form of human endeavor." This knockout line—not in the book—came from Huston as a kind of fresh motto to raise over the script and guide him through it, much as Sam Spade's new-minted "It's, uh, the stuff that dreams are made of" sums up Hammett's theme of greed and illusion.

Both suspense stories choose to take a bite out of our brains and make us face shortcomings we must face if we hope ever to marry our darker with our better natures and become whole. Superbly nimble throughout, these entertainments, each acted to the hilt by performers in top form, carry moral weight and bring new life to the suspense story, and strike us most forcefully with the *Falcon*'s high-flown lines and ironies. A comedy as well as a thriller, *Falcon* satisfies on even more levels than *The Asphalt Jungle*'s gloomy irony. Anybody can be gloomy, but it takes genius to make us laugh no matter how many times we hear Spade tell Gutman, while handing him young Wilmer the killer's guns, "Here, a crippled newsie took 'em away from him. I made him give 'em back"—or watch perfumed and curly-headed little Peter Lorre scream at fat Casper after the falcon proves a fake, raging, "You! It's you who bungled it! You and your stupid attempt to buy it! You—you imbecile! You bloated idiot! You stupid fat-head, you!"

Thieves fall apart—and we are replenished.

Sitcoms leave me brain-dead but when "Roseanne" went into syndication I found myself raptly taping two "Roseannes" nightly, three on Tuesday, for months on end and often watching the same show more than once. Hell, more than twice. The show's writers come and go: a clip of one rehearsal, with the actors in street clothes, revealed Roseanne Arnold tearing out script pages she thought didn't work. The best scenes play with great intensity and some episodes strike so hard that I swear I'm watching something ageless, belly laughs as inspired as Stan Laurel (Laurie Metcalf as longfaced sister Jackie) and Oliver Hardy (Arnold) trying to push a piano over a rope bridge and mid-way meeting a gorilla, Roseanne's husband Dan Conner (John Goodman)—a lunacy underscored by the wisecracks and drolleries of beady-eyed younger daughter Darlene (Sara Gilbert).

My favorite tells about an elderly, warm-voiced door-to-door salesman who asks Roseanne one Sunday morning for a glass of water, then dies at the kitchen table. A Greek-American cop comes and says the body can't be moved until the coroner arrives. That's the opener and the rest turns on the Conner family's discomfort while the sheeted body slumps over the kitchen table all day until the coroner's golf game ends at suppertime. Husband Dan treats the dead man as a microbial leper but must fix the failed food freezer behind the body before Roseanne's rump roast goes bad, and Darlene has committed to making baklava, which the Greek cop helps her bake. Then a husband and wife, answering Dan's ad, show up to buy the laundry dryer he wants to replace, and the wife—a masseuse—gives the dead man a shoulder massage, thinking he's just ill. The police list him as John Doe, but Roseanne's older daughter, Becky (Lecy Goranson), sad that the old fellow who died in their house has to be called John Doe, asks her mother to tell the police his name is William. When morgue attendants finally arrive and start wheeling out the body, Roseanne stops the gurney in the living room and softly and respectfully speaks to "William" under his sheet: "I don't know where you are just now, but if you see Janis Joplin, tell her I still think of her."

With haywire twists I've only hinted at, that tearfully funny script, by Bill Pentland and directed by John Sgueglia, moves fast, with each line and bit of stage business organic to the plot, and unfolds as surefootedly as a Hungarian bedroom farce that time and again reinvests earlier material back into new plotlines, builds to glorious sight gags and to Roseanne's curtain line over the body—which is then topped by a wonderful exit bit. Gruesome? Maybe, but I begin to feel deeply for the warm-voiced dead salesman, whom Dan bitterly nicknames Willy Loman, the suicidal hero of Arthur Miller's *Death of a Salesman*.

The best "Roseanne" scripts depend so fiercely on the actors, who deliver without fail, that they often don't lend themselves to excerpts. One script builds to a long, long silent release full of wordless stage business as Roseanne, a control freak like her mother (Estelle Parsons), falls into the dumps because her wacko younger sister, Jackie, breaks from the fold and goes to the police academy for six weeks, thus escaping Roseanne's critical eye for the first time since her birth thirty-two years earlier. Pretty Jackie's a spinster because Roseanne keeps her under her thumb by shooting down all her boyfriends. The payoff scene comes in Jackie's rugless apartment as she packs to leave. Roseanne has already written her her first letter, and Jackie takes it and reads it to herself, Roseanne seated beside her. The sisters fall into a terrible but silent trembling as Jackie reads to herself, then at last they hug and Jackie leaves. Roseanne follows but first walks about Jackie's apartment, silently picking up messy clothing—a scene lifted from Garbo's great memorial moment in *Queen Christina* where she walks silently about the bedroom she's shared overnight with her lover and touches all the objects in the room so that she'll remember them when he's gone and she's back alone in court. Roseanne sighs her curtain line, "Well, she's a big girl now," and closes the door on her losses.

Silent stage business here becomes heartfelt dialogue.

I stopped writing short stories after publishing my first novel, having found that the gathering power of a novel outweighs the power of a short story and that for me twenty pages of a novel feel far richer than a twenty-page story, with stronger characters and story fibers holding the pages together. The same holds with "Roseanne." With its dour zingers, one episode can carry just so much weight while "Roseanne" as a series carries a huge weight. With the series in syndication, the characters now age before our eyes within weeks, with sprouting Darlene as a clear benchmark. And the quality of the dialogue deepens over the years, as does the playing. As the characters gather body in the writers' minds, deeper drama breaks loose from the family seabottom and floats upward.

Sometimes a writer writes dialogue no actor can fully fill out—words better than they can be spoken, as I said of Shakespeare and of Beethoven's late piano sonatas. One evening on a country road, bare but for a leafless tree, Vladimir and Estragon (Didi and Gogo) wait for a vague figure who never shows. The time of Samuel Beckett's play *Waiting for Godot* (1952) covers two gray evenings. Who is Godot? We never know, nor do Didi and Gogo, two men damned by despair, saved by hope. They go on, they stand still. You can read anything you want into this pair, and for me they carry on a dialogue of body and soul—though to keep us off balance, Beckett at times switches their characters. Gogo seems the body, a donkey or ass, kept alive by a carrot (hope) fed to him by Didi (the soul). Beckett first wrote the play in French and, like God, the mysterious Godot (whose name sounds much like *godillot* and *godasse*, French argot for "boots") will either save them or at last boot them both offstage—if he ever comes. But I'm just noodling. Beckett himself said, "If Godot were God, I would have said that."

As Didi and Gogo wait, two characters, Pozzo and his slave Lucky, pass by and Lucky gives an absurd speech full of punning mock learnedness. The next evening, Pozzo and Lucky pass by again. Pozzo's now blind and being led by a rope Lucky holds while bearing heavy baggage. "I suppose he is Lucky to have no more expectations. . . ." Beckett once said.

VLADIMIR
Where do you go from here?

POZZO

On. *(Lucky, laden down, takes his place before Pozzo.)* Whip! *(Lucky puts everything down, looks for whip, finds it, puts it into Pozzo's hand, takes up everything again.)* Rope! *(Lucky puts everything down, puts end of rope into Pozzo's hand, takes up everything again.)*

VLADIMIR

What is there in the bag?

POZZO

Sand. *(He jerks the rope.)* On!

VLADIMIR

Don't go yet.

POZZO

I'm going.

VLADIMIR

What do you do when you fall far from help?

POZZO

We wait till we can get up. Then we go on. On!

VLADIMIR

Before you go tell him to sing.

POZZO

Who?

VLADIMIR

Lucky.

POZZO

To sing?

VLADIMIR

Yes. Or to think. Or to recite.

POZZO

But he is dumb.

Dumb!

POZO
Dumb. He can't even groan.

VLADIMIR
Dumb! Since when?

POZZO
(suddenly furious) Have you not done tormenting me with your accursed time! It's abominable! When! When! One day, is that not enough for you, one day he went dumb, one day I went blind, one day we'll go deaf, one day we were born, one day we shall die, the same day, the same second, is that not enough for you? *(Calmer)* They give birth astride of a grave, the light gleams an instant, then it's night once more. *(He jerks the rope.)* On!
Exeunt Pozzo and Lucky.

—*Waiting for Godot* (1952),
Samuel Beckett

As Dierdre Bair tells us in her biography *Beckett* (1978), "Beckett himself has said that *Waiting for Godot* is a play that is striving all the time to avoid definition, and as always attention should be given to his words." But let's skip the symbolism of all four characters (there's a fifth, and possibly sixth, character, A Boy, who in his second appearance may be his own brother, as he says he is) and just look at the dialogue.

This starts with a vaudeville turn as Lucky follows Pozzo's commands and loads and unloads, loads and unloads himself. "What is there in the bag?" Vladimir asks. "Sand," Pozzo says, and we may or may not read Lucky's bag as "time"—as in the sands of time. Time is the burden. Pozzo and Lucky often fall down, so Vladimir asks, "What do you do when you fall far from help?"—a wonderful question. "We wait till we can get up. Then we go on," Pozzo says, denying there's help from anyone. Before you go, tell Lucky to sing, just as he quacked us a mock discourse yesterday. Sing? asks Pozzo. "Yes. Or to think. Or to recite." A great request—may we watch him *think*? "But he is dumb," Pozzo says. "Dumb!" "Dumb. He can't even groan." That poor slave can't even groan? "Dumb! Since when?" Vladimir asks. And Pozzo falls into a fury at "Since when?" accusing Vladimir of tormenting Lucky "with your accursed time! It's abominable! When! When! One day, is that not enough for you. . . ." But he calms down and delivers the play's greatest line, about time that is measured in days: "They [days] give birth astride of a grave, the light gleams an instant, then it's night once more." And with Lucky bearing the bag of sand, he cries, "On!"

Waiting for Godot passes the time—it *waits*, the play's stated theme. Autobiographical underpinnings bear out this thought—but they go far afield. What about the language? Certainly "They give birth astride of a grave"— which suggests that babies drop from the womb straight into the grave—hits us as an immense line, powerful as Hamlet's grave mockery of Yorick's skull. Does this tragic abstraction really mean something? Or does Beckett just diddle black notes and dump on us? Depends. The Nobel Prize folks said that Beckett "had transmuted the destitution of modern man into his exaltation." I won't argue. The picture of a woman giving birth over a grave caps his play with a great image. As for Godot—he's Beckett. Beckett is Didi and Gogo, Pozzo and Lucky, and the Boy and his

Brother (who is often beaten by Godot, the Boy tells us). The whole man Beckett seeks in himself awaits the hidden face of the Punisher, who beats the Boy in himself and makes everyone wait while he sleeps. Beckett's vast sleep habit embraced long silences. We are all our characters, we are even Godot, just as the White Whale is one mask of the remote Melville.

Unless you're Beckett or Ibsen, who often spell out everything, a script—whatever its inspiration—becomes only a peg to hang a play on, especially in films and television. Much relies on the actors. Beginning scenarists try to show us every eyebrow twitch and shade of meaning—or camera move. But no two performances of anything turn out alike, and directors laugh at scripts with camera angles. New readings arise, actors get carried away, rehearsed readings fail in the heat of performance. When I was younger I thought that Shakespeare, being hallowed, wrote every scene with a specific dramatic intent that must be played only one way—foolish child! Nothing that depends on actors, the box office, or weekly television ratings can be hallowed—nor is Shakespeare.

In the excerpt below, George Sanders, as theater critic Addison de Witt in the movie *All About Eve*, has all the lines (he's the snake) while Bette Davis, as tempestuous, aging stage star Margo Channing, supports him. Hollywood writer-director Joseph L. Mankiewicz wrote this Broadway dialogue by clashing clichés against stereotypes, hoping by this to ring out some *real* theater chitchat. Robed in fur, Margo exits a taxi and enters the lobby of a theater housing her new vehicle, *Aged in Wood*. There sits Addison in a black lamb overcoat and black homburg and clasping his gloves on his black walking stick, a long black cigarette holder jutting out from his teeth.

MARGO

Why so remote, Addison? I should think you'd be at the side of your protegé, lending moral support.

DE WITT

Miss Caswell at the moment is where I can lend no support, moral or otherwise.

MARGO

In the, shall we say, ladies lounge?

DE WITT

Being violently ill to her tummy.

MARGO

It's good luck before an audition. She'll be all right once it stops.

DE WITT

Miss Caswell got lucky too late. The audition is over.

MARGO

Over? It can't be. I came here to read with Miss Caswell. I promised Max.

DE WITT

Well, the audition was called for two-thirty. It's now nearly four.

MARGO

It is? I really must start wearing a watch, I never have, you know. Who read with Miss Caswell? Bill?

DE WITT

No.

MARGO

Lloyd?

DE WITT

No.

MARGO

Well, it can't have been Max. Who was it?

DE WITT

Naturally enough, your understudy.

MARGO

I consider it highly *un*natural to allow a girl in an advanced state of pregnancy—

DE WITT

I refer to your new understudy, the *un*pregnant Miss Eve Harrington.

MARGO

Eve? My understudy?

DE WITT

Didn't you know?

MARGO

Of course I knew.

DE WITT

Just slipped your mind?

MARGO

How, uh, was Miss Caswell?

DE WITT

Frankly, I don't remember.

MARGO

It just slipped your mind?

DE WITT

Completely. Nor, I am sure, can anyone else present tell you how Miss Caswell read—or whether Miss Caswell read or rode a pogo stick.

MARGO

She was that bad?

DE WITT

Margo, as you know, I've lived in the theater as a Trappist monk lives in his faith. I have no other world, no other life. And once in a great while I experience that moment of revelation for which all true believers wait and pray. You were one. Jeanne Eagels another . . . Paula Wessely . . . Hayes—there are others, three or four. Eve Harrington will be among them.

MARGO

I take it she read well?

DE WITT

It wasn't a reading, it was a performance! Brilliant! Vivid! Something made of music and fire.

MARGO

How nice.

DE WITT

In time she will be what you are.

MARGO

A mass of music and fire. And that's me, an old kazoo with some sparklers. Tell me, was Bill swept away too? Or were you too full of revelation to know?

DE WITT

Bill didn't say. But Lloyd was beside himself. He listened to his play as if it was written by someone else. It sounded so fresh, so new, so full of meaning.

MARGO

How nice for Lloyd. How nice for Eve. How nice for everyone.

DE WITT

She was incredibly modest. She insisted that no credit
was due her. But Lloyd felt as he did only because she
read his lines exactly as he'd written them.

MARGO

You mean I'd not been reading them as written?

DE WITT

To the best of my recollection, neither your name nor
your performance entered the conversation.
[Enter Miss Caswell]
Ahh! feeling better, my dear?

MISS CASWELL

Like I'd just swum the English Channel. Now what?

DE WITT

Your next move, it seems to me, should be towards television.

MISS CASWELL

Tell me, do they have auditions for television?

DE WITT

That's, uh, all television is, my dear. Nothing but auditions.

—*All About Eve* (1950),
Joseph L. Mankiewicz

A neatly written battle of the wasps, though the lines
bear less power than the playing—Sanders won an Oscar
for Addison de Witt. Part of the scene's life comes from de
Witt dropping his armor and unguardedly showing his
highbrow vision of the stage. Even so, he does it in formal
speech. Formal, even with hints of fervor, since stereotypes

must be formal. Would anyone really say, "To the best of my recollection, neither your name nor your performance entered the conversation"? No, he'd say, "Nobody mentioned you"—and carry just as much lofty venom. Reviewers thought Addison de Witt was modeled on theater critic George Jean Nathan, but Mankiewicz said, No, I am de Witt. However, Mankiewicz's sour wit, one of the great prides of Hollywood, dwindled beside the blistering cynicism of his brother Herman, who, eighteen years older than Joseph, won the family's first Oscar by cowriting *Citizen Kane* with Orson Welles. No triumph by Joseph could top Herman's stature as a wit. In this scene, for me at least, de Witt stands for Herman and upstages Joseph's Margo, despite her own edged blade, just as Sanders upstages Davis, never tips his homburg or moves from his seat; he clasps his gloves on his stick and lets his long cigarette holder fume. The stiller he stays, the more we watch him; no matter that Davis keeps busy—and could as well tear her hair out—our eyes never leave the devil trapped in his own bemusement. He moves only to conquer, rising to engage us with his sudden throwing open of the temple door he guards so faithfully. He amuses and moves us as a "true believer"—and we wonder, Does he believe this Trappist monk tripe? Does Mankiewicz? He means it as much as he can mean anything when locked into an aged-in-oak diction that can allow no common utterance to water it.

Noel Coward's *Private Lives* (1930), the very model of brittle worldly wisdom, spoons us romantic nostalgia like so much crunchy *crème brulée*. Elyot Chase, a flip new husband still mooning for his ex-wife, heads the four-character play. By sheer chance, he and new wife Sibyl honeymoon at the same Riviera hotel that ex-wife Amanda and new husband Victor (first played by Laurence Olivier) honeymoon at—and in adjoining suites! Alone momentarily on the first evening of their marriages, Elyot and Amanda discover each other on joined terraces overlooking a moonlit countryside. Though they've been divorced for five years, is it moral for remarried Amanda to take her ex-husband as her lover? The first act ends a bit after this:

AMANDA

What have you been doing lately? During these last years?

ELYOT

Traveling about. I went round the world you know after—

AMANDA
(hurriedly)

Yes, yes, I know. How was it?

ELYOT

The world?

AMANDA

Yes.

ELYOT

Oh, highly enjoyable.

AMANDA

China must be very interesting.

ELYOT

Very big, China.

AMANDA

And Japan—

ELYOT

Very small.

AMANDA

Did you eat shark's fins, and take your shoes off, and use chopsticks and everything?

ELYOT

Practically everything.

AMANDA

And India, the burning Ghars, or Ghats, or whatever they are, and the Taj Mahal. How was the Taj Mahal?

ELYOT
(looking at her)
Unbelievable, a sort of dream.

AMANDA

That was the moonlight I expect, you must have seen it in the moonlight.

ELYOT
(never taking his eyes off her)
Yes, the moonlight can be cruelly deceptive.

AMANDA

And it didn't look like a biscuit box, did it? I've always felt it might.

ELYOT
(quietly)
Darling, darling, I love you.

AMANDA

And I do hope you met a sacred Elephant. They're lint white I believe, and very, very sweet.

ELYOT

I've never loved anyone else for an instant.

AMANDA

No, no, you mustn't—Elyot—stop.

ELYOT

You love me too, don't you? There's no doubt about it anywhere, is there?

AMANDA

No, no doubt anywhere.

ELYOT

You're looking very lovely you know, in this damned moonlight. Your skin is clear and cool, and your eyes are shining, and you're growing lovelier and lovelier every second as I look at you. You don't hold any mystery for me, darling, do you mind? There isn't a particle of you that I don't know, remember, and want.

AMANDA
(softly)

I'm glad, my sweet.

ELYOT

More than any desire anywhere, deep down in my deepest heart I want you back again—please—

AMANDA
(putting her hand over his mouth)

Don't say any more, you're making me cry so dreadfully.

—*Private Lives* (1930),
Noel Coward

Coward and his inspiration for the play, Gertrude Lawrence, recorded a nice swatch of *Private Lives* in 1930. The poor printed lines above give no hint of the trembling richness Coward and Lawrence bring to them. The first act, largely a duologue, runs about forty minutes, and by the time Amanda and Elyot reach these lines, trying every which way to hold back their feelings for each other, their hearts come tumbling out beneath the formality of "Very big, China" while Amanda's idiocies about the Taj Mahal looking like a biscuit box and the sacred Elephant like white lint stanch her feelings like tissues held to a slashed wrist. Behind the actors a string trio plays Coward's "Someday I'll Find You," which Lawrence later sings, saying, "Strange how potent cheap music is." Audiences know that Coward wrote this piece and get a kick out of her putdown. I envy those first London audiences of 1930, with Coward and Lawrence thrilling them to the teeth, and when I hear their recording I see myself at The Phoenix, cheeks wet with delight. Coward tells us in his autobiography, *Present Indicative* (1937):

> Gertie was brilliant. Everything she had been in my mind, when I originally conceived the play . . . came to life on the stage. The witty, quicksilver delivery of lines; the romantic quality, tender and alluring; the swift, brittle rages; even the white Molyneux dress. . . . Our duologue second act when, for some reason or other, we were not feeling quite on the crest of the wave, was terribly exhausting. We both knew that if we let it sag for a moment that it would die on us. On the other hand, when it flowed, when the audience was gay and appreciative, when our spirits were tuned to the right keys, it was so exhilarating that we felt deflated when it was over.

Marcel Carné's film *Children of Paradise* (1944), even at its uncut length of 188 minutes, has a swiftness, beauty, and sophistication unmatched by any other film in any language—or any that I know of. Feelings summoned by art fade with overfamiliarity—and then after long silence may return years later, stronger than ever, more easily summoned. Works ripen. Some books, movies, or plays scorned earlier take on a surprising richness we once lacked the heart to feel. I saw *Private Lives* on stage forty years ago and thought it charming fluff. Now it's a spun-wire castle of nerves and nuance—at least on the Coward-Lawrence thirties recordings—and I envy the high laughter and prickly joys Coward wrings from its pages. And I admire the pacing, the short, fast speeches that rip toward a payoff in the moonlight. Much the same, I found Marcel Carné's *Children of Paradise* a dreadful romance in my judgmental early twenties, though I liked much of the acting and Jean-Louis Barrault's miming. But what a terrible script! I could have done so much better.

Ah, well. Jacques Prévert's script for *Children of Paradise* today? The very peak of sophisticated screenwriting! Filmed largely in Nice during the changeover from Nazi Occupation to the Liberation, the story begins in 1840 and tells of the love carried by France's greatest mime, the moon-born Baptiste Debureau (Barrault), for Garance (Arletty). But Baptiste idealizes her too greatly—their affair remains fruitless, not even an affair. Indeed, for the four male leads in the film, the distant Garance embodies four distinct types of perfection. She becomes the mistress of haughty Count de Monteray, while Baptiste marries Natalie (Maria Casares), the stage manager's earthbound daughter who idealizes him. Six years pass, Baptiste and Natalie have a son, the mime becomes a practical man of the theater. At last, Garance and Baptiste meet again, at an after-theater party, and go off to a moonlit garret where they had once failed to perfect their love bodily. This night they make love. "Love is so simple," Baptiste says. "Yes, when you love each other!" she says. Next morning, their door opens and his wife, a surprised Natalie, finds them dressed but embracing. Natalie apologizes, saying she thought she'd find Baptiste alone in this old garret of his. As she stands there, we wish she'd leave, but she holds her ground, pleading for him to speak to her and dispel her embarrassment. She once interrupted Garance and Baptiste at a similar moment six years ago before marrying Baptiste. Now that ghastly moment returns and slaps her in the face.

BAPTISTE

Natalie!

NATALIE

Is that all you can say?

(Garance moves to leave but Natalie shuts and blocks the door, face to face with Garance.)

NATALIE

No!

GARANCE

I assure you I must go. [Indeed, she must stop a duel that is to be fought over her.]

NATALIE

Again! . . . How easy it must be!

GARANCE

What must be easy?

NATALIE

Easy to go away . . . and then to come back, missed. Time works for you and you come back, all fresh, and made more beautiful by memory. Oh, yes, that must be easy! But to stay, and live with one man, to share with him the ordinary things of everyday life, that's something else. Yes, that's something else. And you can do nothing against that. Six years, do you hear? Six years I've lived with him.

So have I.

NATALIE
(dumbfounded)

You too?

GARANCE

Yes, me too. Anywhere, everywhere, every day . . . and
even at night, all the nights I spent with someone else,
all those nights I was with him . . .

BAPTISTE
(disturbed and embarrassed)

Garance!

NATALIE

Let her go on, I want to know everything about you two.
Yes, I want to know what is left for me . . . if you have
left me enough to live on . . . And after all, what does
it matter whether you love him or not? You don't
count . . . you don't exist for me.
(Entreating, she takes Baptiste by the shoulders)
Baptiste, listen to me, answer me; don't be afraid to
make me suffer. Suffering's not very important, everybody does it. But I want to know, I want you to reply to
me immediately, do you hear! Look at me; were you
always thinking of her while you lived with me? Oh!
You daren't even reply!
(Garance slips out)
But you tell me a lot by keeping silent . . . and I understand . . . I understand what you don't say.
Baptiste brutally frees himself and rushes out after Garance.

—*Children of Paradise* (1944),
Jacques Prévert

That scene—the wounded wife facing in the flesh her
husband's erotic ideal, his rape of their marriage, and the

possible abandonment of her and her child—plays with heavenly depths on the screen, and Casares and Arletty imbue their characters with stainless nobility, neither being in the wrong. The viewer faces impossible moral choices and Baptiste has no lines that affect the argument. Why not? Because he must await the outcome as these two faces of his soul battle for him. Garance leaves him to his earthwife, but "brutally" he still chases after the ideal, releasing in us strong, deep, wonderful pain—feelings that refresh.

Amazingly, this face-off—Baptiste pulled apart by love for his earthwife and child and for his moonlit fuck from heaven—appeared only when the filmmakers felt something seemed to be missing from the plot and decided at the end of shooting to improvise this moment of moral choice. Though filmed flatly in a small space, the immense restraint in the acting turns the lines to ringing silver—a duel between the injured wife and the eternal mistress unmatched on screen for truth-telling. Remember, this flick runs three hours and eight minutes with no intermission; the hour hand marks the third hour and we are ready for the story's payoff. These lines *must* hit us like Scarlett's "Rhett, what shall I do!" and Rhett's "Frankly, my dear, I don't give a damn"—in fact, many viewers call *Children of Paradise* the French *Gone With the Wind*. Prévert's lines touch depths far beyond Rhett's and Scarlett's, yet feed our hearts' hunger just as theatrically. And in both cases, the men split, although Baptiste may never again bed Garance and must certainly return to Natalie.

How does the scene work? First, Natalie refuses to leave, having too much to lose and too many unanswered questions: she stands there, emotionally raped by the lovers. And we feel it as she pleads, "Oh, please don't leave me [standing here] like this, all alone, it's so awful. . . ." Think about it. Your wife stands there, crushed, abysmal, do you say something to relieve her or not? Helpless, he says only her name. So she lights into Garance instead. How easy it must be for you to go away for six years and come back glamorized by memory, she tells her. Ah, but to stay and put his food on the table and bear his child and put up with his baffling whims as an actor and character, while losing six years of your youth, that's something else. Six years, do you hear? I've lived with him six years.

Her eyes certain but her mouth sad and dreamy with those six years *without* him, Garance says, "So have I."

"You too?"

"Yes, me too. Anywhere, everywhere, every day . . . and even at night, all the nights I spent with someone else, all those nights I was with him. . . ."

And from what we know of moonstruck Baptiste, the glory of whose artistic sensitivity now rules the Funambules, the gutter stage where pantomime looms supreme, we know Garance does not understate the spell of his image. Life without Baptiste stands still emotionally.

Baptiste tries to break in but Natalie says, "Let her go on, I want to know everything about you two. Yes, I want to know what is left for me . . . if you have left me enough to live on." And anyway, Natalie adds, she doesn't exist for me [not as she exists for you]. Her love doesn't matter, doesn't count.

But Garance shoots her bolt with her exit line. She slips out as Natalie begs Baptiste for the truth: "Don't be afraid to make me suffer . . . Look at me; were you always thinking of her while you lived with me?"

And Prévert inspiredly has the frozen-faced mime say nothing while his wife reads his glittering shame.

Ahh!

Then he throws her aside, her strength drained, and races after the wild duck of beauty, love, and freshness flying away with his heart. But the carnival-roaring street, packed with Baptistes, gutter folk costumed as the famous mime's Pierrot, floods against him and he can't reach her through waves of Baptistes carrying him away from her. Carl Jung, did you adore that shot?

David Hare scripted his play *Plenty* for the 1985 film directed by Fred Schepisi and starring Meryl Streep among a fabulously gifted cast. Streep plays Susan Traherne, an Englishwoman whose great moment comes during World War II when—at seventeen!—she works with Britain's Special Operations Executive and carries out acts of subversion and sabotage behind enemy lines in occupied France. Now, the war over, England foresees a world of plenty—yet rots from within. So does Susan, who—though intelligent, beautiful, and hard-willed—finds herself so unfulfilled and her powers put to such poor use in a stupefying donkeylike society that she has a series of nervous breakdowns. Susan's jobs hold her but briefly. When overseeing dinnerware for the Queen's coronation, she buys some spoons from a black marketeer with a lower-class accent, Mick Halloran (Sting). She sends him a letter to meet her at the Embankment, near a bridge on the Thames. He comes but first tries to sell her five hundred cheese graters for the Coronation. She turns this down, yet bathes him in a warmly inviting radiance.

MICK

So, you better tell me how I can help.

SUSAN

Well, I'm looking for a father. I want to have a child.

Look, it really is much easier than it sounds. Marriage is not involved, or even looking after it. You don't even have to see the pregnancy through. Conception would be the end of the job . . . You don't want to?

MICK

No—no, I'd be delighted. I'm lucky to be asked.

SUSAN

Not at all.

MICK

It's just, uh, your own people, friends—you must have friends.

SUSAN

I'm afraid I'm quite strong-minded, as you know. The men that I've met at work or my friends, as you'd say, they usually feel that I'm holding myself in—that I'm literally blowing them out of the room. They are kind, they are able, but I don't see why I should have to compromise. I don't see why I should have to make some sad and decorous marriage just to have a child. I don't think any woman should have to do that.

MICK

You don't have to get married. You just go off with 'im. You don't tell 'im!

SUSAN

Ha ha! Yes, I did think that. But then I thought it would be dishonest. So I had the idea of asking someone I barely knew.

MICK

I'd really like to know why you chose me. I mean, how often have you met me?

SUSAN

That's the whole point.

MICK

With Alice a few times. I'm clean, obedient, haven't got any morons in the family.

SUSAN

It's not as calculated as that.

MICK

Not as calculated as that? Several hundred of us, was there? All got notes, did we? Sayin' come and meet me at the Embankment, tell no one, bring no friends. I thought with all the secrecy you must want nylons.

SUSAN

I'll buy nylons, if that's what you want.

MICK

Why me?

SUSAN

I like you.

MICK

And?

SUSAN

I love you? I chose you because I don't see you very much. Barely ever see you. We live at opposite ends of town. Different worlds.

MICK

Different class.

SUSAN

That comes into it.
[He sells her 500 cheese graters.]

It can't be what you want. Not deep down.

SUSAN
No. Deep down I'd do the whole damned thing myself.
So there you are, you're second best.

> —*Plenty* (1985),
> David Hare

This scene plays mostly in close-ups and close two-shots, and Sting's sly but respectful mug against the rose glow of Streep at peak sexuality adds measureless life to the images and lines. Rousing light stirs beneath Susan's all-business face in becoming a mother, a flame whose cool sexiness wavers in her flesh like light through candlewax. During the lines above, a wordless, kissless kiss between her and Mick, their mouths and noses dancing toward and away from a joining that never comes, goes on seemingly for an entire minute. Meanwhile, a political subtext also lies under the lines and under every scene in the script. But let's leave that for the English to spell out.

What makes this scene play? First, the unusualness of a ravishingly feminine woman (who rises to the upper class) asking a mug to knock her up—and paying him too, despite his delight at the offer. And we know as well that he's her best friend's sometime lover. Then her saying that members of her own class, well, they're so blown away by her that she needs a man like Mick who will stand up for himself intrigues us. She wants to keep a certain mental keenness and wholesome honesty about this purposeful sex act. "I chose you because I don't see you very much. Barely ever see you. We live at opposite ends of town. Different worlds." In fact, deep down, she wishes she could do the whole damn job herself. No dependency. Throughout the script an independent Susan means a sane Susan, and the more dependency she falls into with the foreign service officer she marries, the less sane she becomes. So, as dependency eats away the English spirit, we watch it break Susan's spiritual self-support but in no way blunt her sensitivity and mental agility. Also, we remember throughout that the wellspring of her spirit first overflowed when faced with the life-threatening danger and ever-present fear of torture during the war. At that time, though a teenager, she disguised herself for years as Suzanne Marchaise and thought and acted as a mature French woman. At one point she was the only member of her network who hadn't been caught. When the war ended and she came home, she found it hard, even peculiar, to speak freely in English. Though we viewers may make allowances for a hardheadedness and mental problems that seem less genetic than rooted in wartime experiences, the script never does. Hare never sentimentalizes. Whatever Susan's problems, they're hers, not his— though, as playwright, he gave them to her. Her basic problem remains that postwar life does not measure up to her old life underground and the swelling energies of a dangerous disguise. Being Susan Traherne again, whoever civilian Susan is, robs her deepest being—and there's no answer for this slow rot and emptiness that eats up her young dreams of plenty. And Streep plays these losses stingingly.

To play the alcoholic street bum Helen Archer in William Kennedy's script of his Depression novel *Ironweed* (1987), as directed by Hector Babenco, Streep adopts staggering physical changes, a new musculature and skeletal structure, and a voice out of a cistern. Eyes misted and teeth bent and yellow, she hobbles about as if with stones in her shoes. Helen once had a classical piano radio program on which she sang as well, and long ago played abroad on concert tours in Paris and Vienna—at one point in the film she goes into an Albany piano store and plays Chopin (it's clearly Streep playing). She and her paramour, Francis Phelan (Jack Nicholson), both have mental problems from booze—she talks to herself on the street and Francis often sees white-suited spooks, some men he killed without meaning to. He also killed a baby son by dropping him on the kitchen floor after a few beers. His guilts hang like chain, while Helen's genteel past trails cobwebs in the breeze. They sleep on cardboard in empty buildings, though cold weather sometimes demands she sleep in an abandoned car in a junkyard and meet her fat host's need for a handjob. Francis takes for granted that she does this.

One cold night in 1938, chilled to the bone, Helen and Francis visit his wino friend Jack, who has a job and shares his rooms with Clara. By midnight they're all drunk on Jack's muscatel, and he tells Francis and sharp-tongued Helen to leave—"Clara's sick." Actually, he and Clara can't stand Helen, who often shouts when drunk. Jack makes Francis a cheese sandwich and the two guests leave by the back stairs, going down to an alley shadowed by lamplight.

FRANCIS

Now where in the hell *you* gonna sleep!

HELEN
(very fast)

I wouldn't stay there they gave me silk pillows and mink sheets! I remember her when she was whoring—and always BROKE! I had to speak my mind, that's all.

FRANCIS

You didn't accomplish anything. Here, have a piece of sandwich.

HELEN

Ugh! It'd choke me. [She has a stomach tumor.]

FRANCIS

It won't choke ya. You'll be glad for it.

HELEN

I'm not a phony.

FRANCIS

I'm not a phony either.

HELEN

You're not, eh?

FRANCIS
(screaming)

I'LL SHOW YOU WHAT I'M GONNA DO! *(Grabbing her collar and her throat, screaming into her eyes)* I'm gonna knock you across that goddamn street! Now be a god-damn woman! That's why you can't find nowhere to flop. I asked for a sandwich—did I get it?

HELEN
(reeling but standing up to him)
Yeah-h! You're stupendous—and colossal!

FRANCIS

Don't you SQUINT your eyes at me or I'll knock you over that goddamn automobile! You been a pain in the ass for nine years!—Jack told me that I could stay—but *you* can't because you're a pain in the ass! They don't want you! Now I'm gonna eat this sandwich!

HELEN

I can't eat it.

FRANCIS

Jesus wept. *(throwing the sandwich into her face)* Here you are, woman, eat this.

HELEN

I won't eat it. It's rat food.

FRANCIS
(banging her against wall, down to her knees)
I'm gonna kill you! Don't drive me insane! Now be a goddamn woman and go the fuck to bed somewhere.

HELEN
(up and hoity-toity)
I'm gonna call my brother! HAH!

FRANCIS

Good. Why don't you call him twice so he can hang up on you again? Where you gonna get a nickel for the call?

HELEN

That's my business. You were all right until you started on the wine! *(Suddenly sobbing)* WINE! WINE!

FRANCIS
(holding her)
I'll get some cardboard. And we're gonna go down to that old building.

HELEN

I'm going on down below.

FRANCIS

Who you kidding? You got nowhere to go. You want to get knocked over the head?

HELEN

It wouldn't be the worst thing that ever happened to me! YOU'RE GONNA HIT ME NOW! *(She sobs.)*

FRANCIS

I'm not gonna hit ya. I love ya some, babe. Don't go walkin' away from me, you'll get lost in the world. *(She laughs, snuggling.)* You awful cold?

HELEN

Yeah. *(He gives her his suitcoat.)* I couldn't stay out tonight, Francis, I'd die.

[They stagger up the lamplighted alley together, arms about each other for warmth in the midnight hour, pals.]

—*Ironweed* (1987),
William Kennedy

Bullheaded, rock-bottom drunks, their nerves stripped bare, aflood with anger, yet both striving for dignity despite the madness tossing them about. Searing stuff—one of the greatest scenes ever filmed. Nicholson roars from his bowels, shakes and bangs Streep all over the alley, knocks her down, throws his sandwich straight into her face when she's down, and yet she sticks her jaw right into his, weeping, shouting back hoarsely, "YEAH-H! You're stu-PENDous—and colossal!"

Their lines stick close to the novel's dialogue for this scene but rise in intensity, being cut by a third and kept to the alley rather than to a walk Helen and Francis take looking for sleeping space. The actors pound on their lines like wild horses, mangling one or two—Streep's "silk pillows and mink sheets" should be "silk sheets and mink pillows"—but that hardly matters before the blistering power worked up.

The scene kicks off explosively and stays at that pitch until the final minute, when their madness passes, he gives her his coat, and they go off into the night holding each other, with a few lingering notes of the old music-hall song "He's My Pal" trailing after them on the soundtrack—a song Streep sings movingly in an earlier scene. The scene builds to Helen's accusation, "You were all right until you started on the wine!" and then her sobbing, "WINE! WINE!" which catches Francis's ear. That rare bird, an honest drunk, he hears the truth in her cry. And his madness dies. Does the dialogue ring true, or perhaps ring with the tin ear of Eugene O'Neill's drunk talk in *The Iceman Cometh*? Well, it's better drunk talk than O'Neill's. To me "silk pillows and mink sheets" sounds forced, but may simply be an unfamiliar idiom, while "Don't walk away from me, you'll get lost in the world" strikes me as odd, if not sentimental. Once again, such quirks fade before the firehose performances. Whatever its flaws, inspired dialogue makes possible great moviemaking. The critics didn't agree—but these performances will outlast us all by centuries. Remember my young man's takes on *Private Lives* and *Children of Paradise*? Took me forty years to get my head straight.

Greta Garbo had no such problem with the critics when *Camille*, brilliantly directed by George Cukor, drew gasps and tears in 1936. Everyone said Garbo'd hit her peak, just as they should see Streep's Helen Archer as a peak performance. Both actresses had great lines. Garbo's three scenarists, Frances Marion, James Hilton, and Zoe Akins, handle Alexandre Dumas fils's old warhorse of a play skillfully and give her dialogue from the heavens of romance.

In this scene she plays the aging kept woman, Marguerite Gautier, who when chased by very young Armand Duval (Robert Taylor) turns away his attentions—there's more money in Baron de Varville, who, indeed, now supports her. She falls ill (tuberculosis!—the great romantic illness of the nineteenth century), but springs back and happens to meet Armand at a house auction in Paris. In the library he hands back a handkerchief she once planted for him to find. "And you kept it with you all this time? *Always* with you?" she asks. "Always with me. Like an old friend, to remind me that I'm not the Baron de Varville." That's not a very romantic reason, she complains, and he says, no, he keeps it as a warning against romance.

MARGUERITE

How sensible. *[Barely noticeably, she coughs, digs away in her purse for a pastille.]* Has this made you very cynical? Is that why you've never taken the trouble to call on me?

ARMAND

Perhaps.

MARGUERITE

I'm sorry. One needs friends.

[Enter NANINE, Marguerite's elderly maid, bearing Marguerite's cape.]

NANINE

I've been looking for *you*. Oh, Monsieur, you can see for yourself she's quite well again. Well, or would be if she took proper care of herself.

MARGUERITE

Why do you think my health would interest M. Duval, Nanine?

NANINE

Because he came every day when you were ill to ask how you were and to leave flowers.

MARGUERITE
(big pause)

He's the one?

57

NANINE

Tell her yourself, Monsieur! He just said a friend, so I thought—

MARGUERITE

All right, Nanine. Wait for me downstairs.

NANINE

Yes, Madame. *[Exit]*

MARGUERITE

You might have asked to see me.

ARMAND

Well, I—I knew there were so many others.

MARGUERITE

There were no others. None, during all those weeks the doctors thought I might die.

ARMAND

Not even the Baron de Varville?

MARGUERITE

Baron de Varville chose to be in England at the time. No, you were the only one who took the trouble to ring my bell.

ARMAND

But now?—

MARGUERITE

Oh now, I'm well again and all goes merrily! Would you care to come to a party I'm giving tomorrow night? It's my birthday! *[Cough]*

ARMAND

Aren't you afraid you're not strong enough yet to give parties?

MARGUERITE

Oh, I'm afraid of nothing but being bored. It's supper—after the theater.

ARMAND

I'll come with pleasure. And I'll bring this little book as a birthday present. Have you read it?

MARGUERITE

I never read anything. What is it?

ARMAND

Manon Lescaut.

MARGUERITE

Who was she?

ARMAND

A beautiful girl who lived for love and pleasure.

MARGUERITE

It's a beautiful color. It should be a very good story.

ARMAND

Yes, it is. But it's rather sad. She dies in the end.

MARGUERITE

Well, then, I'll keep it but I won't read it. I don't like sad thoughts. However, we all die. So perhaps this will be sold someday at an auction after my death.

ARMAND

I thought you didn't like sad thoughts.

MARGUERITE

I don't! But they come sometimes. Au revoir, M. Duval.

ARMAND

Goodbye.

—Camille (1936),
Frances Marion, James Hilton, and Zoe Akins,
from the novel and play *La Dame aux Camellias* (1852)
by Alexandre Dumas

Delicately, Garbo builds Marguerite's bad lungs into the script with this bittersweet tossing aside of her fatal illness. But she will die at home, in her lover's arms, not of thirst in the desert like Manon Lescaut. A half-heard cough and tiny rap on her breastbone, the soft rifling in her purse for a tin of pastilles, pass by almost unnoted, as does her leaning against a wall to save strength. From this foreshadowing, tragedy arcs over the film—but here the heartache begins, in Garbo's wry smiles and brilliant eyes, which mask her nineteenth-century AIDS.

The lines foreshadow as well, and Garbo's throwaway reading of them drives death in like a tent stake when the foreshadowing comes. "I'll keep it but I won't read it. I don't like sad thoughts. However, we all die. So perhaps this will be sold someday at an auction after my death."

That Armand kept her handkerchief on his person all these months, and that, as Nanine tells her, he was the nameless but faithful well-wisher who left flowers for her daily when she lay near death, with little hope that he would ever see her again, well, such worship from a divine youth moves her—but not deeply. She doesn't like deep feelings, sad thoughts, or reading books. She likes birthday parties. Even when Armand confesses his love at the birthday party, she says, "Well, what can I do about it?" and pins a camellia into her hair. (A white camellia once signaled sex for hire, a red camellia the monthlies.) Her turning here from an affair with the handsome innocent—delaying any fun but his company—adds a smoky flavor to the tragedy. She's too wise to put herself through a wringer for young Armand. And yet—her heart demands that she feed this adoring youngster! How can you do this to him! Armand's father later cries at her. "Monsieur," she says, "what if I tell you that I shall not live very long?"

Greta, I thought you didn't like sad thoughts?

"I don't! But they come sometimes. Au revoir. . . ."

Let's jump from Meryl and Greta to Marilyn Monroe at her best, in *Bus Stop* (1956) and *The Prince and the Showgirl* (1957), roles filmed within the same twelve months. In the first, Marilyn plays a waif from the Ozarks with a poor to fair singing voice ("Thayut old blayuck ma-agic hayus me in its speyull. . . .") who aspires to the respect given to café society singer Hildegarde. Unlike Giulietta Masina, who played the Chaplinesque waif of Fellini's *La Strada* (1954), Marilyn's waif keeps an innocent heart but learns from experience. Her director in *Bus Stop*, Joshua Logan, an old Broadway wizard, thought her the best actor he'd ever directed and set her beside Chaplin. The through-line of her feelings in the first scene below lies in her thirst both for discovery as a singer and respect as a person. In this dressing-room scene she works as an entertainer/bar girl at the Blue Dragon Café in Phoenix, Arizona. The accomplished stage actress Eileen Heckart, as Vera, supports her in the role of Cherie and marvelously shrinks herself into a far less hopeful and smaller mind than Cherie's—no easy job!

CHERIE

He called me an ignorant hillbilly! How do you like that?

VERA

Well, ain'tcha? I don't mean ignorant, I mean, but ya do come from th' Ozarks.

CHERIE

I ain't done hillbilly since I was—well, not since I turned chanteuse.—I been tryin' to *be* somebody. *[Burying her disgust and face into her hands in her dresser mirror, then looking up pleadingly:]* Can you imagine if Hildegarde was

61

jumpin' down between her numbers, sittin' in some truckdriver's lap?

CHERIE

VERA

I don't know why ya just don't quit.

CHERIE

I can't! Look! *[opening her purse]*—I don't get paid till Wednesday. Owe for my room an' everything. Besides that, it took me too long to get this far. *[Showing Vera a map from her purse]*

VERA
(studying a red crayon line on the map)
What's that line for?

CHERIE

That line? You might say that this line here is the picture of my life. See that there where it starts? That's River Gulch, the little ol' town where I was born.

VERA

River Gulch, I never ever heard of it.

CHERIE

Well, it ain't there any more anyway. Floods came and washed us all away, except me and my baby sister Nan. I just picked her up and took her along here, this line *[pointing at map]*, until we got to Lubbock, Texas. D'ya know what happened there! Nan got this job waitressin' and I worked in Liggett's drug store. *And* this amateur contest opened and Nan said to me, Honey, why don't you enter yourself in that contest? You been watchin' people in movies—then I used to live in the movies— you been watchin' people put over their songs and *ges-*tures, you know? So, I did it. An' I won it!

VERA

Furst prize?

CHERIE

No, second prize. Couple of boys juggling milk bottles won first prize. Anyway that's how I got my direction an' all.

VERA

Direction?

CHERIE

Oh sure! If you don't have a direction you just keep goin' round in circles. And look [pointing at red line on map], this is just how straight my direction is. River Gulch, that's where I *started*, this is where I am *now*—and look where I'm *going*.

VERA

Where?

CHERIE

Hollywood and Vine! Look, straight as an arrow, *phshew-w!* —Hollywood and Vine!

VERA

Ha ha! What happens when ya get there?

CHERIE

Honey, you get disCOVered! TESTED!—with options— *everything!* And you get treated with a little respect too.

—*Bus Stop* (1956),
script by George Axelrod,
from the play by William Inge

Josh Logan weighs Cherie as half-Inge and half-Axelrod and shaped entirely as a role for Marilyn. She plays throughout in what might be called clown off-white makeup, which looks even whiter when she's seated beside three-years-younger Hope Lange on a nighttime bus ride. As with Giulietta Masina's Gelsomina in *La Strada*, this clownish color shores up Marilyn's pathetic image below the conscious mind as we watch. She's a three-dimensional drawing come to bosomy life, and with eyes and mouth that catch the finest passing feelings. Hold this in mind when reading the lines above, which set up visual effects as strong as—or stronger than—the lines themselves. Cherie's entrance, above, brings a burst of light and life to a thin first act. Before us in a window sits unbelievable loveliness fanning herself in a lazily silken bird-of-paradise dressing gown. Marilyn's energies rise to a high glow playing Cherie's despair with the galoots of the Blue Dragon Café and then changing into her shabby dancing outfit with its burst fishnet stockings. When she speaks, out comes this Texas-Oklahoma twang that Marilyn has mastered and turned into an actor's day at the beach. She knows every syllable of the script and comes on entirely in character as her boss shakes her like a ragdoll and tells her to get out to the customers. Her first line: "He called me an ignorant hillbilly!" "Well, you are, ain'tcha?" Vera asks, and we believe it.

The scene falls into three emotional areas. It opens with Cherie crushed by her boss and digging self-worthlessly at her blonde frazzle—and shows as well her thwarted yearnings to be a café society singer—and remains with her defeat until she takes out the map—her magic lamp. Just see how the red crayon line drawn across it boosts her spirit. Her face floods radiantly as she makes clear the great journey she's on from River Gulch to Lubbock to Phoenix. Then the scene lifts off for the moon as she tells us she's goin' straight as an arrow to *Hollywood and Vine!*

Vera too laughs, carried away by Cherie's feelings, and asks, "What happens when ya get *there*?"

And Cherie erupts with dreambubbles. "Honey, you get

DISCOVERED, TESTED—with OPTIONS—*EVERYTHING*! And ya get treated with A LITTLE *RESPECT* too."

This, of course, reminds us that years earlier we all asked ourselves, How can this wiggling, tongue-tied young heifer expect ever to be an actress?

The Prince and the Showgirl finds Marilyn as a far more polished entertainer, who dances skillfully, hauntingly sings "I Found a Dream," and has aged a few years beyond Cherie. Where the scene above from *Bus Stop* offers Cherie to us in a monologue broken up by Vera, her straight man, Marilyn's Elsie Marina finds her pitted against a real force, a great actor who is as well the film's director. The film opens in 1911 on the eve of the coronation of George V and Queen Mary. The Regent of Carpathia (Olivier) attends a stage show and invites an American showgirl for a midnight supper in the Carpathian embassy. The story varies "Sleeping Beauty" in that the Regent is—as Terence Rattigan's original play was entitled—*The Sleeping Prince*, a man emotionally frozen and given to medicinal but mechanical easy lays. Only a kiss by one who loves him can wake his sleeping heart. Elsie comes to supper in a pure white evening gown into which she's been poured like cream, her ripe bosom and pouting tummy and rounded bottom a fantasy of curves that could waken stone. All during the so-called two-person dinner, she eats alone while he conducts political business on the room's phone. When he decides that she's been fully fed and drunk enough vodka, he makes his move.

REGENT

My dear, wouldn't you be more comfortable on the sofa? You could put your feet up and rest.

ELSIE

I think I'll stay here, thank you.

REGENT

Very well. Just as you please.
(pause)
My dear, it was so good of you to come and see me here
tonight.

ELSIE
(nervously)

You said that before.

REGENT

Did I? *(kneeling beside her, his palm hovering over her bosom)*
That is a beautiful dress.

ELSIE

You said *that* before too.

REGENT

(amorously)
What does it matter? What are words—
*(With practiced movement he rises and swings round onto the
arm of Elsie's chair, encircling her waist as he does so)*
—where DEEDS can say so much more!
*Elsie jabs him hard in the stomach with her elbow, and jumps
out of the chair.*

ELSIE

That's just terrible!

REGENT
(catches falling monocle, holds his stomach)

What is terrible?

ELSIE

That performance of yours.

REGENT
(aggrieved)

I fear I do not altogether understand you, Miss Marina.

ELSIE

Now don't pull that Grand Duke with me. You made a pass, I turned it down. That's all that happened. We can still be friendly.

REGENT

Excuse me.
(goes to drinks table, tosses vodka cork aside)

ELSIE

Say, listen. I could use a short one.
The Regent, without replying, pours another glass and hands it to her.

ELSIE

I need it for my heart. It's kind of beating down here.

REGENT
(stiffly)

I am so sorry.

ELSIE

Oh, it's not your fault. In fact if I'd known this was all that was going to happen, I wouldn't ever have been nervous.
(pause)
Well—long life to Your Grand Highness.

REGENT
(automatically)

Cheerio.
Throws drink to the back of his throat, as does Elsie.

ELSIE
(naughtily)

And better luck next time—only not with me, of course.

Say—there *is* something to this stuff, you know. Are you sure it has no effect when you drink it that way?

REGENT

After three of them, you might experience a certain euphoria. I think you have had enough.

ELSIE
(getting muzzy)

I think so too. I don't know why I was so nervous tonight . . . I thought I was going to have a real struggle with myself. I thought—well, of course, I would have won it—I always do. But I thought, This time he's a Hungarian prince and Your Grand Ducal. Well, with fire and passion and—I thought if anyone knows about this love stuff, this guy will. Ha ha ha! I even thought—I even thought that you'd have *gipsy* violins somewhere outside and that the *lights* would be low and that there'd be a strange seductive perfume everywhere in the air. Well, put it all together, I thought, hm, sister, you better watch your step, you just better watch out! Oh, well— Do they all fall as easily as that, those Maisie Springfields and all those others?

—*The Prince and the Showgirl* (1957),
Terence Rattigan

The scene plays rollickingly and the two actors tear into it with relish. The whole seamless show, in fact, plays like a dream and never hints at the difficult shoot many reporters say took place. Seamlessness comes hard, added to which Marilyn had a miscarriage during the shoot, telling no one, and wound up in therapy with Sigmund Freud's daughter Anna. Olivier, who'd played his role onstage, reads his lines letter-perfectly, but Marilyn Americanizes hers and reads them better than as written.

This scene works for four effects: the erotic tension (his hand hanging over her bosom) leading up to the Regent's big move ("What are words—where DEEDS can say so much more!"), Elsie's fighting him off and then her relief as she explains her nervousness, the Grand Duke's icy silence at being rebuffed, and then Elsie's muzzy champagne-and-vodka aria about the big struggle she foresaw she'd have when a Hungarian prince tried to seduce her into that love stuff, with gipsy violins, dim lights, and perfume.

This gives the prince ideas and he sets about fulfilling her dreams, with fiddles, dim lights, and perfume.

I make much of the actors here because Rattigan wrote the play as a light soufflé for the coronation of Elizabeth II and not as anything "serious." Let it be whatever the actors make of it. Onstage, Olivier kept his role toned down so Vivien Leigh, his none too stable wife, would shine more brightly as Elsie. In the film he finds unscripted but terrific business for himself in every frame—self-amusedly shooting a footstool to Elsie with his boot, angrily throwing the vodka cork aside, a glacial mask in place for the first two acts until Elsie "awakens" him. Marilyn, in turn, gives so much body to her presence, and such appeal and innocence to her reading, that this piece of lighthearted kitsch becomes eternal art.

By now you may be saying, Don, this is all very well, but how do you get to write dialogue for Greta Garbo, Meryl Streep, Marilyn Monroe, Laurence Olivier, Marlon Brando, and Jack Nicholson? Isn't this just, well . . . a pipe dream for your readers? Exactly! And please treat it as such. We're here to empower each other to dream big. So just stoke up and read on *as if* writing for Garbo or Brando or Streep. Or Marilyn. Or Jack or Sir Larry.

But you want to get serious? All right. A few more very

choice bits of dramatic dialogue, then we'll move on to stuff whose authors control every inflection, no actors in sight.

Akira Kurosawa directed the great film *Ikiru* (1952) and wrote it with co-scenarists Shinobu Hashimoto and Hideo Oguni. *Ikiru* means "to live" in Japanese. It tells of Kanji Watanabe (movingly played by Takashi Shimura, more famed for his next role as the top samurai in Kurosawa's classic *The Seven Samurai*), a middle-aged petty bureaucrat and widower who spends his life walled up in offices. We first see him at his desk with a sea of string-bound papers rising behind and around him. All life has left him; he sits mechanically stamping forms with a wooden seal or rebuffing petitioners who want him to fight City Hall and get their parks and water supply cleaned up. He's dead but doesn't know it. In fact, the picture opens with an X-ray plate of his stomach and the narrator telling us that Mr. Watanabe has gastric cancer. It's odd that a picture about dying is called *To Live*? No! The story's about living.

Once Watanabe gets the deadly news from his doctor, he slips into limbo and spends the first night of the last six months of his life crying in bed. His job now means nothing, nor do his ties with his money-loving son and daughter-in-law. He chooses to set forth on a life of pleasure. In a dark sake shop he meets a lowlife writer of cheap novelettes—played with showy grunginess by Yunosuke Ito, costumed in a Bohemian black hat, black coat, and long scarf—a devil's word-shoveler fresh from his inkwell. He will be Watanabe's guide in the world of pleasure. The Writer offers him a whiskey.

WATANABE
No, I can't . . . I'd just throw it all up. I have gastric cancer.

WRITER
(concerned)

Cancer?

WATANABE

Yes.

WRITER

Then you shouldn't drink this.
He puts his hand on Watanabe's shoulder.

WATANABE

I don't really want to talk about it . . .

WRITER

But to drink, knowing that you have cancer . . . it's like committing suicide.

WATANABE

No, it's not that easy. I'd thought of ending it all, but it's hard to die. And I can't die just yet. I don't know what I've been living for all these years.

WRITER

Do you have any children? *He receives no answer.* Well, does your stomach hurt?

WATANABE

More than my stomach, it's . . . *He presses his chest.*

WRITER

But there must be some reason for all this.

WATANABE

No, I'm just a stupid fool, that's all. *He pours himself a cup of sake and drinks it.* I'm . . . well, I'm angry with myself. Up until a few days ago I've never spent anything on drinking. It was only after I found that I didn't have much longer to live that I . . . *He pours himself more sake.*

71

WRITER

I understand, but you still shouldn't drink. Does it taste good?

WATANABE

No, it doesn't. *He puts down his cup.* But it makes me forget. I'm drinking this expensive sake now because . . . well, because I never did before. It's like drinking poison. I mean, it seems like poison, yet it's so soothing. *He smiles.*

WRITER

I see what you mean.

There is some food on the table which Watanabe has not eaten. He sees a black dog, drops the food on the floor, and the dog bolts it down.

WATANABE

I have about fifty thousand yen with me. I'd like to spend it having a really good time. But, and I'm ashamed to admit it, I don't know how to. If you would . . .

WRITER

You're asking me how to spend it, to show you how?

A train passes very near, shaking the stall and making the bottles rattle.

WATANABE

Yes, that is what I wanted to ask you to do.

WRITER

But—

WATANABE

It took me a long time to save this money, but what I mean is that now I can spend it.

WRITER

I understand. Look, keep your money. You'll be my guest tonight. Leave it all to me . . . You know, you're very interesting. I know I'm being rude, but you're a very interesting person. I'm only a hack writer, I write trashy novels, but you've made me really think tonight. *He pours himself a glass of whisky.* I see that adversity has its virtues—man finds truth in misfortune; having cancer has made you want to taste life. *He drinks the whisky.* Man is such a fool. It is always just when he is going to leave it that he discovers how beautiful life can be. And even then, people who realize this are rare. Some die without ever once knowing what life is really like. You're a fine man, you're fighting against death—that's what impresses me. Up until now you've been life's slave but now you're going to be its master. And it is man's duty to enjoy life; it's against nature not to. Man must have a greed for life. We're taught that that's immoral, but it isn't. The greed to live is a virtue. Let's go. Let's find that life you've thrown away. Tonight I'll be your Mephistopheles, but a good one, who won't ask to be paid. *He looks down at his feet.* Look, we even have a black dog!

—*Ikiru* (1952),
Hideo Oguni, Shinobu Hashimoto, and Akira Kurosawa

The two men go forth seeking pleasure, play pinball, buy Watanabe a new hat, go to a dance hall, a beer hall, a strip show. But Watanabe throws up. No pleasure can soothe cancer.

So Watanabe tries to help a bouncy young girl from his office and devotes himself to her happiness. This too passes. Watanabe tells himself, "It is too late . . . No, it isn't too late. It isn't impossible . . . I *can* do something if I really want to." And watching a toy rabbit hop on his restaurant table as he hears nearby children sing "Happy Birthday," he feels reborn by their voices and an idea inspired by the toy.

He will use the power of his office, feeble though it be, to reclaim a wasteland and make a playground for children. Happy birthday, Mr. Watanabe.

At that point the picture breaks in half. Five months later, we go to Watanabe's wake with his family and office staff. The keenly realistic first half of the film fades as the staff and family members recall a false Mr. Watanabe—not the Watanabe we know. True, looking back through the eyes of those at the wake, we watch him build his park, while dying, at great personal cost, fight the bureaucracy, the underworld, greedy politicians, and so on. We know Mr. Watanabe died fulfilled—but no one else knows! Only Watanabe himself, now gone, knows that he died spiritually whole. And as the illusions of others cover him over, he truly dies, buried in the living.

Jesus, that's wonderful.

Watanabe's night drinking with the Writer takes us deeper into his dilemma, strips him of common pleasures, and sets him up to lose family love and dusty job satisfactions. By midpicture nothing remains of Watanabe but himself, and here the wormlike bureaucrat—no props left—achieves the freedom, decision, and commitment to become the hero who proves himself to himself. At the time Kurosawa made the picture, existentialism raged through Western thought: life means only what you grant it to mean, and what you make of it. Did Kurosawa have this in mind when he and his fellow scenarists wrote the script? Makes no difference. The picture says just this, with no word for an afterlife. You gotta do it all right here—on the planetary hardpan. You might even suck some joy into your limbs if you dredge your waste, break up your clay, offer yourself up as compost in a garden for life—or, like Watanabe, build a playground as your body rots.

Grow greedily or die ignobly. It's up to you.

The scene excerpted moves very slowly and Kurosawa says in his autobiography that Takashi Shimura plays it too heavily, all stops out. Kurosawa would have liked Shimura a little more relaxed, but blames only himself for not having told his actor this. So we get Shimura's reading of the scene, not the writer's, even though the writer directs. In their next film together, *The Seven Samurai*, Kurosawa gets Shimura to show shining irony through his mask as the wisest samurai. Throughout *Ikiru* Watanabe only grins lopsidedly at his own shortcomings and remains ever more intensely humorless until his fade-out on the playground swing. Would the last scene be stronger if he'd lightened up earlier? The lines in the sake shop give him little leeway. In this case, did the actor know better than the writer-director? Well, when an actor gets out there and delivers, he has to go past the written word.

Writing and acting demand different talents. Most writers of dramatic dialogue know this and hope that the actor will bring even greater bloom to the bare beauty of their lines. Kurosawa wrote this script at age forty-two after having fallen into brown thoughts about his own death. In it he's all his characters, the hack writer (drawn in part from Kurosawa's own feelings as a studio slavey and script-writing assistant director for seven years), the striving Watanabe, the short-tempered people opposing him, and all the others. He tells us in *Something Like an Autobiography* (1982) that among his own works, *Ikiru* and *The Seven Samurai* remain his two favorite films.

Dennis Potter wrote two masterful British television series, *Pennies from Heaven* (1981) and *The Singing Detective* (1989). In both scripts, Potter shows great invention while often moving us, in part by springing old recordings on us.

In a fairly recent talk on British television, he says that he does not use old songs for nostalgic effect but rather to highlight something alive in the characters. He dislikes nostalgia, he says, it locks you into the past with no hope of explaining the present. But songs from the past, he says, hang about in our heads as part of our current baggage; at times they have a brightness that sheds light on the present. When Arthur Parker, his Depression-era song-sheet salesman in *Pennies from Heaven*, gets into unbearably dismal troubles, he finds himself singing to an old recording, "Life Is Just a Bowl of Cherries"—which for Arthur it sure ain't. Mysterious!—but no bowl of cherries. These are rather grim lyrics ("You can't take your dough when you go-go-go"), while the title song's lyrics ("So when you hear it thunder don't run under a tree") become quite poignant when Arthur speaks them, without music, a hangman's noose around his throat.

Potter's six-hour masterpiece, *The Singing Detective*, tells the story of the long hospitalization of middle-aged detective–story writer Philip Marlow (Michael Gambon), now in a London ward for his umpteenth eruption of psoriasis and crippling arthritis, his entire body covered with painful, itchy red peeling, his joints too stiffened and aflame for him to scratch anywhere. His skin breaks and burns whenever he moves, and high fever keeps him dreaming in hell. When we first see him, a stretched-out, lightly boiled lobster, paralyzed with pains no drug can reach (more a live lobster on the boil), soft background violins play "I've Got You Under My Skin." This may seem easy irony, but the "You" in the song title ties into Marlow's spiritual desolation with his faithless wife and his misused writing talent as well as with his illness, and release from desolation becomes his goal.

Marlow denies that his illness springs from his mind, but the script says something else, as does Potter in a BBC-TV interview. A cynic of Shakespearean blackness with a violently bitter gift for poisonous abuse, Marlow lies hallucinating, his crazy temperature freeing ragged bits of the past that mix with a new novel writing itself in his mind—he can't light a cigarette, much less hold a pen. His mind writes on unbidden, and we switch from Marlow bedridden to Marlow's hero in action—that private eye known as The Singing Detective because he sings in cafés as well as detects—and then to nine-year-old Marlow back in his coal-mining home village. Marlow the child greatly loves his father, who sings for money and stuns customers at a pub with rapturous birdsong imitations whistled through his fingers. Mother backs him up on the piano. But Mother, disgusted by their home life with Dad's parents (the grandfather has black lung disease and hawks phlegm to sizzle on the stove lid), takes a lover and Philip comes upon his dressed and bestockinged mother on her back and fucking a bare-assed man in the woods. Her guilt becomes his, and when he hallucinates about his mother, his wife replaces her and fucks the same man in the woods his mother fucked. Also, through cowardice, Philip once snitched on a fellow student, who then got caned. More guilt. And severe writer's block, despite his fever dreams, adds to his stress. Once his problems overwhelm him, the psoriasis hits and— apart from whatever caused it—runs its own course; its severity and sudden terrors create their own weakening fears and run down his resistance and deepen painfully its inflaming his arthritis and the likelihood of its return. With his face so badly disfigured and the disease ragingly acute, Marlow looks "as though boiling oil had been thrown over him."

We learn from the interview, quoted later, that Potter himself suffers from this illness—but he denies and is offended by the suggestion that Marlow's an autobiographical character. I have the illness, Potter says, but not Marlow's bitterness. Marlow can not understand himself enough to tie in with his feelings. His enforced bed-stay gives him a world of time for probing parts of his soul as wounded as his body. His fever recasts his problems as a Singing Detective story, set in the thrillerish fogs and café lights of 1945, in which all his guilts and fears arise in new masks—a puzzling dreamnovel he goes on sifting when awake. Meanwhile, his real wife (whom we first see as Marlow's mother fucking in the woods) visits him on the ward—and one could get lost in these time-and-storyline shufflings. On first viewing, his series' sheer bravura entrances us; a second viewing allows us to sink past his method and more richly into Marlow's soul—what's left of it.

One morning, during rounds by callous consultants and a visiting doctor who see him only as a specimen, Marlow boils over. He says nothing as they dissect his case. At last, breaking down, he begs them to listen to him:

MARLOW

The thing is—the thing—I—listen!—I can't—I've reached the end—

CONSULTANT

Oh. Of what?

MARLOW

My tether . . . I'd like—Christ, I'd—like to get out of it. I don't want—I can't—listen—I can *not* stand it really truly can not stand this any more. I can't get on top of it or see clear of it or think straight or—or—tell what is

from what isn't—and—*(Rising panic)* And if I don't tell someone, if I don't admit it—I'll never never get out of it, never beat it off and nevernevernever—
He is laughing, half crying.
Tears even bloody useless tears, sorry about, shame of, even tears oozing bloody useless, hurt the—ooh the skin on my face and—hee! hee!—laugh—ooh it hurts my jaw and God! Talk about the Book of—the Book of Job I'm a prisoner inside my oooh own skin and and and bones—
He suddenly stops, worn out, ashamed, stiff and still.

Marlow lowers his mask at last and in this blistering monologue speaks of his suffering, although only a minute earlier he has insulted the doctors as "slobbering cretins—who turned out to be escapees from the local loony bin. They thought they were doctors and nurses." But despair overcomes him. Tears burn his skin if he cries, his jaw hinge flames if he laughs. He's Job, "a prisoner inside my oooh own skin and and and bones—"

Michael Gambon falls apart, wailing, and yet remembers every syllable of his lines during this outburst, giving Marlow a majestic despair much like Job's after his disasters. This man has no way out of his intense, hellish, night-and-day pain. Even so, lodged in his monologue, as befits a detective story, lies the clue to his salvation. He must lower his mask and admit his pain, not just clamp it under with vile ironies. These defeat all hope. "If I don't tell someone, if I don't admit it—I'll never never get out of it . . ." He may be P. E. Marlow, creator of that wisecracking ironist The Singing Detective, who cannot afford to let one true feeling escape his lips, but he's also Philip Marlow, victim of psoriatic arthritis, who needs to speak out and let the world in if he's to recover. That's the monologue's clue.

But the hard nut pulls back into his shell. Taken on an enforced visit to "the cuckoo man," Dr. Gibbon, the hospital psychiatrist, Marlow hoses Gibbon with his worst ironies. Coolly, Gibbon says, "This is an act. This is desperate pastiche."

Gibbon's got hold of a copy of *The Singing Detective* pulp magazine and read it, searching for clues to Marlow's bulletproof ego. Marlow thwacks him over and over, but Gibbon smiles grimly. At last he points to the hidden fear and loathing of sex in P. E. Marlow's writing. Marlow jeers, "My God. Oh, my God. This is so-o-o sick."

But Gibbon soon reveals a second clue to Marlow's recovery, should it ever be, and tells him, "The skin, after all, is extremely *personal*, is it not? The temptation is to believe that the ills and the poisons of the mind or the personality have somehow or other erupted straight out on to the skin. 'Unclean! Unclean!' you shout, ringing the bell, warning us to keep off, to keep clear. The leper in the Bible, yes? But that is nonsense, you know. *Do* you know? Well— one part of you does, I'm sure."

The clue, of course, lies in his mother's and wife's unfaithfulness and his hunger for love while thinking it unclean since he was nine years old. And not only unclean, but deadly in a horrible vast way that has murdered his God-like, bird-whistling father, turning his spirit to stone just as Philip now turns into a burning statue whose slightest movement speeds flames from hell.

Dr. Gibbon asks Marlow plainly, having read his prose, "My feeling is that you did not set out to write like that— What sort of things would you rather have written about?"

"If I had the talent, do you mean?" Marlow asks, then answers with a glib roulade. But Gibbon's not satisfied.

Marlow stares. And then, all at once, mysteriously, some sort of hostility, some level of tension, seems to leave him.

MARLOW

I would have liked to have used my pen to praise a loving God and all his loving creation.

DR. GIBBON

Really?

MARLOW
(Gratingly)
Moreover—I would have liked to have seen hosts of radiant and translucent angels climbing along spinning shafts of golden light deeper and deeper into the blue caverns of heaven . . .

—*The Singing Detective* (1989),
Dennis Potter

This reply knocks us over, since Marlow has not spoken from the heart—except once about his pain—since we met him. But we catch the bump of the true poet rising from his split brow and know that his burst of spiritual feeling roots itself in his cuckolded father's power to fill rooms with the God-given glory of his bird-whistling. Gambon's ecstatic rapture on these lines rings true. Philip Marlow, his father's son!—who buries his gift in shit. Said too much, Marlow thinks, and slips quickly back under his armor.

I've given my ideas on these passages as we went along. Now I'd like to quote Potter himself about his script. British television interviewer Alan Yentob first reviews excerpts from many Dennis Potter television specials over the past twenty years, then asks him, "How do you present your convictions [rather than your more cynical views]?" Potter answers:

> Principally by showing or attempting to assert how sovereign you are as an individual human being if you knew it . . .
>
> What I'm trying to do in *The Singing Detective* is to make the whole thing a detective story but a detective story about how you find out about yourself. So that you've got this superfluity of clues, which is what we all have, and very few solutions, and maybe no solution. The very act of garnering the clues and the very act of remembering not merely an event, but how that event has lodged in you, and how that event has affected how you see things, begins to assemble a system of values and only when that system, no matter how tenuous it might be, is assembled was Marlow able to get up out of his bed. Which is why it isn't about psoriasis or arthopophy or detectives or that particular childhood but about the way that we can protect that sovereignty that we have, and that is all that we have, and is the most precious of all those human capacities, even beyond language—it is almost impossible to talk about it because you are bumping against the very rim of communication when you try to talk about it. But being able to use the musical conventions and the detective story conventions and the autobiographical conventions, and making them co-exist at the same time so that the past and the present weren't in strict sequence—because they aren't—they are in one sense obviously in the calendar sense—but they're not in your head in that sequence. And neither are they in terms of the way you discover things about yourself, where an event twenty years ago becomes more—it can follow yesterday, and so precede it. And out of this morass, if you like, of evidence, of clues, and searchings

and strivings, which is the metaphor for the way we live, we can start to put up the structure called Self. We can walk out of that structure saying, "At least I know and you know better than before what it is we are."

—Dennis Potter,
1989 interview

Potter bumping against the very rim of communication strikes me here as a kind of genius, able to speak from strength about a being's sovereignty. Felled as often as Marlow, and full of the monkish self-searching he uses to bead the string of his plot, he lays open his most subjective creative parts with striking thoughtfulness and lets them speak. We're not used to such fine self-analysis in television interviews—this out-Mailers Mailer. Is this sovereignty stuff real, or half-baked? Is Potter fudging about his script's deepest sources? Note that he avoids the objective about his script, his cliffhanger episode endings and so on. Frankly, I can see how Potter has a strong conviction of self we might call sovereignty, much like George Bernard Shaw's, and I *like* the way his interview sentences mirror the tricks of *The Singing Detective* itself, with the sense often hanging fire as you await more clauses or sequences. Both Potter and his script strive to ask fearless questions about themselves and not settle for half-truths. I envy his sense of play as a writer—and what must be a fabulous collection of old wax discs. I should mention that Potter did not create Marlow's voice out of thin air but did a run-through on the crime novel in two wonderful thrillers he wrote just before this script, *Blackeyes* (1987) and *Ticket to Ride* (1986). I quote the opening sentence of *Blackeyes*:

The lovely Jessica sat alone at a small white table in front of a smaller white page, and although she looked so neat and demure there was murder in her heart.

Actually, P. E. Marlow writes with far more purple in his Singing Detective novels:

Mouth sucking wet and slack at mouth, tongue chafing against tongue, limb thrusting upon limb, skin rubbing at skin. Faces contort and stretch into a helpless leer, organs spurt out smelly stains and sticky betrayals. This is the sweaty farce out of which we are brought into being. We are implicated without choice in the slippery catastrophe of the copulations which splatter us into existence. We are spat out of fevered loins. We are the by-blows of grunts and pantings in a rumpled and creaking bed. Welcome.

In *Man and Superman* George Bernard Shaw speaks of his most serious religious belief: the Life Force in Evolution. As an essay, his thoughts will have a small audience. So he dresses them up as a comedy—and the play is still playing. Acting groups sometimes drop the third of its four acts as not part of the main story. But the third act, called *Don Juan in Hell,* sees the boards as a one-act play far more often than the full play, *Man and Superman.* So Shaw both wins greatly and loses a bit on this venture. All who see *Don Juan in Hell* delight in its fantasy and play of ideas. Those who see the four acts in their entirety (and I have) come away wrung dry by their ideas.

Shaw calls Don Giovanni by his original Spanish name, Don Juan, and adds his own fantasy to Mozart's opera as Juan chooses for a while to rest and think on hell's border. Who should arrive from earth but Dona Ana—whose father Juan killed while trying to seduce her—now dead of old age. Her late father, today Juan's friend, walks about as a self-admiring statue. These three fall into a long chat with the Devil, who wants to keep them bound to him by the pleasures of hell. But Juan states that he must leave—he believes in the Life Force and can't stay in this sty of self-delusion. Rather, he wishes to give himself to the purposeful Life Force, which he thinks a part of Nature.

THE DEVIL

You think because you have a purpose, Nature must have one. You might as well expect it to have fingers and toes because you have them.

DON JUAN

But I should not have them if they served no purpose. And I, my friend, am as much a part of Nature as my own finger is a part of me. If my finger is the organ by which I grasp the sword and the mandoline, my brain is the organ by which Nature strives to understand itself. My dog's brain serves only my dog's purposes; but my own brain labors at a knowledge which does nothing for me personally but make my body bitter to me and my decay and death a calamity. Were I not possessed with a purpose beyond my own I had better be a plowman than a philosopher; for the plowman lives as long as the philosopher, eats more, sleeps better, and rejoices in the wife of his bosom with less misgiving. This is because the philosopher is in the grip of the Life Force. This Life Force says to him "I have done a thousand wonderful things unconsciously by merely willing to live and following the line of least resistance: now I want to know myself and my destination, and choose my path; so I have made a special brain—a philosopher's brain—to grasp this knowledge for me as the farmer's hand grasps the plow for me. And this" says the Life Force to the philosopher, "must thou strive to do for me until thou diest, when I will make another brain and another philosopher to carry on the work."

What is the use of knowing?

DON JUAN
Why, to be able to choose the line of greatest advantage instead of yielding to the direction of least resistance. Does a ship sail to its destination no better than a log drifts nowhither? The philosopher is Nature's pilot. And there you have our difference: to be in Hell is to drift: to be in Heaven is to steer.

THE DEVIL
On the rocks, most likely.

DON JUAN
Pooh! which ship goes oftenest on the rocks or to the bottom? the drifting ship or the ship with a pilot on board?

THE DEVIL
Well, well, go your way, Senor Don Juan. I prefer to be my own master and not the tool of any blundering universal force. I know that beauty is good to look at; that music is good to hear; that love is good to feel; and that they are all good to think about and talk about . . . But if you should change your mind, do not forget that the gates are always open here to the repentant prodigal. If you feel at any time that warmth of heart, sincere unforced affection, innocent enjoyment, and warm, breathing, palpitating reality—

DON JUAN
Why not say flesh and blood at once, though we have left those two greasy commonplaces behind us?

—*Man and Superman* (1903),
George Bernard Shaw

To Don Juan, Man is Nature in contemplation of itself, certainly an appealing thought, though it fails to say whether Nature is the sum total of forces at work in the universe, or simply the material world about us. If he means the second, then Nature uses man to mark off its space in the heavens and becomes a somewhat superman or superthinker, just as curious about the universe as man is curious about Nature. Juan's great speech and the Devil's parries move lightly but bear spirited thought. Even the Devil's offerings come from the heart as for one last time this great seducer tries to lead Juan aside from higher goals and blur him with food and warm, breathing, palpitating flesh.

What do I think about the thoughts in the Life Force speech? They woke me up forty years ago and have filled my lungs ever since. When the actor playing Don Juan hits that speech, and brings humanity and wit to his reading, it thrills the mind. And then comes the strong support of the drifting log versus a ship-with-a-pilot argument. Juan wins the battle but not without intensely amusing attacks by the Devil. Shaw well knows that without a powerful Devil to tilt against, the Life Force will not shine, and so the Devil has a powerful "force of Death" speech which begins, "Have you walked up and down upon the earth lately?" and then spells out the refined weapons of war that Evolution and the Life Force have produced through Man. He might better have asked how life can feed on life without horror, or how the Life Force can use evil as a humus for greater, more intensely hungering life, the suggestion being that God eats his own body. A keen arguer, Shaw prided his own disinterest in playwrighting as an art and used the stage as a pulpit for ideas. Dramatized ideas. "I write plays with the deliberate object of converting the nation to my opinion. . . . I have no other effectual incentive to write plays. . . ." he said. His heroes—like Henry Higgins in *Pygmalion* and its musical adaptation, *My Fair Lady*—shine as heartless thinkers and reasoners. "Why can't a woman be more like a man?" becomes a serious question for Shaw, which he answers with the idea that eventually she must breed a Superman for the Life Force. Of himself Shaw says, through Juan, "I tell you that as long as I can conceive something better than myself I cannot be easy unless I am striving to bring it into existence or clearing the way for it. That is the law of my life. That is the working within me of Life's incessant aspiration to higher organization, wider, deeper, intenser self-consciousness, and clearer self-understanding."

Should his spirit sound *too* inhumanly intellectual, Shaw tells us earlier, in the play's dedication:

> This is my true joy in life, the being used for a purpose recognized by yourself as a mighty one; the being thoroughly worn out before you are thrown on the scrap heap; the being a force of Nature instead of a feverish selfish little clod of ailments and grievances complaining that the world will not devote itself to making you happy.

That moves me.

Samson Raphaelson (1896–1983), the greatest writer of sophisticated comedy ever to hit Hollywood, worked on nine films with Ernst Lubitsch, a distinguished director of disarmingly warm comedies. Their two finest films together, *Trouble in Paradise* (1932) and *The Shop Around the Corner* (1940), still play on television, can be rented, and I foresee the globally linked electronics by which you or I might bring up on a screen any film in this book and go to the very lines I write about, if these scenes are not already gathered for us—and I may live to see it!

A New York playwright from Chicago, Raphaelson worked on scripts with Lubitsch and early on mastered comic turns as infolded as the Hungarian farce—say, his wildly twisting plot, repartee, and outlandish stage business about pickpockets in *Trouble in Paradise*. Let me excerpt the climax of *The Shop Around the Corner*, Raphaelson's film rewrite of Miklos Laszlo's light comedy *Parfumerie* (originally *Illatszertar* in Hungarian). Though more a warmly sincere comedy than a triumph of artifice, Raphaelson's script floats with a faintly bittersweet perfection whose taste brings joy, though a failed suicide arises midway. Between world wars two lonelyhearts, Klara Novak (Margaret Sullavan) and Alfred Kralik (James Stewart), become amorous pen pals by way of their numbered post boxes. They never meet and don't know each other's name. Then Klara lands a counter job selling novelties and leatherware in a sizable Budapest gift shop, the very store in which senior clerk Kralik rises to manager. Full of dreamfluff and pretenses, Klara does not hit it off with the serious Kralik, who did not want to hire her in the first place.

Christmas Eve they meet in the back room of the gift shop. He shows her a gold necklace he's bought for his fiancée, which Klara genuinely admires, and tells her that *her* fiancé came to see him. "You shouldn't have told him who I am. I spent a very uncomfortable hour. He apparently didn't believe it when you wrote him I meant nothing to you."

Under her questioning he goes on to describe "Mr. Popkin" and adds, "Personally, I think that little tummy of his gives him a nice homey quality." Popkin's also "balding," "somewhat depressed," and out of work. She defends

"Popkin" manfully, or at least hopefully, until Kralik adds, "He feels you both can live very nicely on your salary."

KLARA

That's terrible! I'm outraged! I never dreamed he was materialistic like this! If you read his letters—such ideals—such a lofty point of view! I could quote you passages . . .

KRALIK

What, for instance?

KLARA
(thinks a moment, then quotes)
"To love is to be two and yet one—a man and a—"

KRALIK

"And a woman, blended as an angel—Heaven itself!" That's by Victor Hugo. Popkin stole it.

KLARA
(heartbroken, sits on empty box)
I thought I was the inspiration of all those beautiful thoughts—and now I find he was just copying words out of a book! And he probably didn't mean a single one of them!

KRALIK
(very sympathetic, sitting beside her)
I'm sorry you feel this way. I hate to think I spoiled your Christmas.

KLARA

I built up such an *illusion* about him. I thought he was so *perfect*.

KRALIK

And I had to be the one to destroy it.

KLARA

That's all right. I—I really ought to thank you.
(She gets up.)

KRALIK
(getting up, too)
Klara, if I had known in the beginning how you really felt about me, things would have been different. We wouldn't have been fighting all this time. If we did quarrel, it wouldn't have been over handbags and suitcases, but something like—should your grandmother and your aunt live with us or not.

KLARA
(wrecked but brave)
It's very sweet of you to try to cheer me up like this, but I think we'd better say good night. You have an engagement—and so have I. And we shouldn't be late. *(She gives him her hand.)*

KRALIK
(taking her hand and holding it)
You know what I wish would happen? When your bell rings at eight thirty tonight and you open the door—instead of Popkin, *I* come in.

KLARA
(suffering)
Please—you're only making it more difficult for me.

KRALIK
(ardently beginning to embrace her)
And I would say to you, Klara, darling—

KLARA
(fighting it)
Please don't!

KRALIK

Dearest, sweetheart, Klara—I can't stand it any longer.
Please get your key. Open postbox two thirty-seven.
Take me out of my envelope—and kiss me.

KLARA
(struggling)
No, Mr. Kralik, you mustn't—

She suddenly realizes that he knows about the postbox—
the exact number. And he has quoted from one of her
letters. She stares at him as at a ghost. Kralik takes a car-
nation out of his pocket [their signal] and puts it in his
buttonhole.

KRALIK
(in a trembling voice)
Dear Friend! *(She leans back against the counter, looking at
him again and again.)*

KLARA
(trying to get it into her head)
You—Dear Friend?

KRALIK
(not too sure of himself)
Are you disappointed?

KLARA

Psychologically I'm very confused—but personally I
don't feel bad at all! . . . Tell me—when you came to the
cafe that night, I was pretty rude to you—

KRALIK
(dismissing it)
Aw—

—*The Shop Around the Corner* (1940),
Samson Raphaelson

A failure-proof scene!—as witty but richly felt as that Hungarian Franz Lehar's superbly plotted 1905 operetta, *The Merry Widow*, which to my knowledge has had only one bad performance since opening night.* And Lubitsch and Raphaelson add a few more lines to set up an amusing fade-out.

Whatever you think about this scene, its airy current of human feelings caught up in a soft flame redeems any flaws. Though set in Budapest, its most Hungarian quality lies in the respectful way Miss Novak and Mr. Kralik address each other. The paprika's quite mild, though Lubitsch sustains a slight Middle European flavor throughout. Stewart and Sullavan hit their lines strongly in character, playing less for romantic Hollywood comedy than for a humanity that allows us to join the heartfelt release these two enter so perilously. The lines wait like soft chamois gloves for the actors to slip into—and there's no rush getting the gloves on. When will lines like these come again?

The scene turns on the first line of the excerpt as Klara at last gives up on "Popkin." Then comes the charm of Kralik quoting Popkin's theft from Victor Hugo. Klara cries, more to herself than Kralik, "I built up such an *illusion* about him. I thought he was so *perfect*." Then Kralik begins the long apology we know will pay off for him—*if* this throaty-voiced, odd, deliciously high-minded frail bird of a blond doesn't go berserk. We've seen her faint before. She fights his ardency, but his knowledge of her post box number and ease at quoting from her letter bring the dawn. "She stares at him as at a ghost." That's fabulous. A wide-open stage direction telling the actor to Take It Big. And Maggie does.

"Dear Friend!" His heart sizzles in the frying pan.

"You—Dear Friend?" Still can't believe it.

*Herbert von Karajan's Deutsche gramophone studio recording—after a spirited overture, a train wreck that goes nowhere.

"Are you disappointed?"

Ahh, how could she be, life doesn't often hold up a full platter like this.

A beat, then she releases the vaulting line that frames her character: "Psychologically I'm very confused—but personally I don't feel bad at all!"

You should rent this.

America's most original comic genius in films remains writer-director Preston Sturges, who cut his teeth on Broadway, then on Hollywood scripts, before becoming a writer-director at forty-two and in a four-year period giving us four or five comedies whose crests of farcical nuttiness he could never again match—nor has anyone else. But comparisons are fishy. Let's just say *The Lady Eve* (1941) stands out as his least absurd but most lastingly well-made romantic film farce—though flawed by a faint dip in the third act from which it quickly recovers.

In *The Miracle of Morgan's Creek* (1944), Norville (Eddie Bracken), a small-town bank clerk, can't get into uniform—he has high blood pressure, and during times of stress, black spots dance before his eyes. Trudy Kockenlocker (Betty Hutton), Norville's dream girl, likes uniforms. One night, to get around her grouchy widower father, she has Norville take her "to the movies"—she drives instead to a servicemen's farewell dance in Norville's car while he fumes in the movie house. She doesn't come back to the theater until eight in the morning—Norville still waits out front. Drunk, she can't remember anything about the dance. We know that while jitterbugging crazily at the dance, she'd hit her head on a chandelier and been given free champagne—then come out of a blackout driving home alone, a curtain-rod ring on her marriage finger. She's married a soldier whose face and name she can't remember—neither of them gave their right name to the justice of the peace—and he's shipped out. She's also pregnant.

In this tender scene from the early middle of the picture, Trudy and Norville, a small, homely, shy schnook, long in love with Trudy, who stammers when upset, walk from her front porch through town in a beautifully detailed tracking shot that lasts well over five minutes without a cut as they pass storefronts and turn corners and cross this and that small-town street. This may be the best scene Betty Hutton ever played, tears battling restrained hysteria while Trudy tries to hook Norville as a husband to save her reputation. They walk, walk, walk, and midscene she decides she can't deceive him—he says he'll marry her—and makes a clean breast of it:

TRUDY

I'm married.

NORVILLE

You're married, well that's—you're WHAT!?

TRUDY

Norville, don't get carried—

NORVILLE

Trudy, you said said—Oh, excuse me, I thought for a minute you said you were married.

TRUDY

I did say I was married.

NORVILLE

You did say you were mar—YOU DID SAY YOU WERE MARRIED! TRUDY! You—*the spots*—said you were married!

TRUDY

It happened that night.

NORVILLE

It happened that night?—YOU MEAN THE NIGHT YOU
WERE OUT WITH ME?—Trudy, that's the—

TRUDY

That's right.

NORVILLE

Trudy, that's the terriblest thing I ever—How could you
do—*the spots!*—to me?

TRUDY

That isn't even the worst of it.

NORVILLE

That isn't even the—WHAT COULD BE WORSE THAN
THAT?

TRUDY

You're gonna make me cry!

NORVILLE

Well, go ahead and cry all ya like, see if I care!—*the
spots!*—Who did ya marry?

TRUDY

I don't know.

NORVILLE

You don't know. YOU DON'T KNOW!? Whaddaya mean
you don't know? That's the most ridiculous statement I
ever—I—I—I—

TRUDY

His name had a Z in it—I *think*—I don't know. I've
thought so much about it. The more I think about it the
less I can remember. And don't tell me to find the name
in the marriage license, because I haven't got any! And
don't ask me if I'm sure I'm married, because I am sure!

NORVILLE

How can you be sure if there's no name on the r-r-r-record? How can you p-p-p-possibly be su—TRUDY!—[It dawns on him.]—Dya mean—

TRUDY
(sobbing, whispering)

That's right.

NORVILLE

THE SPOTS!—Oh, that's terrible! I feel terrible.

TRUDY

How dya suppose I feel?

NORVILLE

Well, that's the terriblest thing I ever—what's your father gonna say when he finds out and ya can't—I mean, and ya haven't any husband—any proof! I mean, any—WHO'S HE GONNA—[think did it? Trudy looks at Norville the Seducer.] THE SPOTS!

TRUDY

I can almost see them myself.

NORVILLE

How-how-I'm the LAST person—I tried—

TRUDY

Try to focus!

NORVILLE

F-focus!

TRUDY

You better take me home, Norville.

NORVILLE

F-focus!

No, home.

H-h-hocus.

—*The Miracle of Morgan's Creek* (1944),
Preston Sturges

In 1944 seeing a Hollywood comedy about a pregnant minor seemed as likely as being served a boiled frog for Sunday dinner. Film critic James Agee suggested that the Hays Office, which censored scripts and demanded revisions, had been "raped in its sleep." For me, this scene—it's many pages longer—finds Sturges at his most humane and glowing. Any actors could work wonders with these lines, but Hutton and Bracken would not likely be bettered. Hutton especially sucks the viewer far into her suffering, with Bracken, the leaping, falling, stammering clown beside her, a straight man for Betty's rich, smiling, silent pain. To me, she and Bracken form one character in Sturges's mind, with hopping Norville acting out Trudy's anguish. Pain glows as the through-line of the scene, though the lines themselves hardly hint at it. So what can you learn from this? Be your own director! Or hire actors whose readings—or whose cry THE SPOTS!—can give more pathos to a scene than you thought you'd written into it.

Well, you might say, Woody Allen matches Sturges as a writer-director. True! And I can't praise the dialogue or anything else of Sturges in top form more than that of Allen in top form. Allen, in fact, often reaches farther and presses harder than Sturges and can strum the heartstrings until they ache, as in the last scene of *The Purple Rose of*

Cairo (1985) or the last scene of *Manhattan* (1979; lifted from Chaplin's *City Lights*, 1931) or with the poignance of the Waldorf lobby scene in *Broadway Danny Rose* (1984), where Danny's client drops him for a bigger agent. So, I take back what I said about Sturges being matchless. Agh, such fish.

In the Depression-era color film *The Purple Rose of Cairo*, a waifish, naive Cecilia (Mia Farrow)—married to thuggish, out-of-work Monk, who mooches off her baby-sitting pay and waitress's tips—escapes everyday dreariness by watching Hollywood romances at the Jewel Theater. Fired from her waitress job and in despair with her home life, she goes to the Jewel at noon one day and sits through the black-and-white *The Purple Rose of Cairo* three times although she's already seen it twice the day before. This *Purple Rose*, a swank drawing-room comedy, amuses us as a silvery film within the color film. Suddenly in the midst of a scene, Tom Baxter (Jeff Daniels), explorer, archaeologist, and son of the Chicago Baxters, spies Cecilia in the audience ("My God, you must really love this picture") and walks out of the screen and off the stage to talk with her. This astounds Cecilia much less than it does the society folk in the black-and-white film on screen, who see one of their members desert them. (Actually, Tom himself should remain in black and white since he has never known color.) He hustles Cecilia out a side exit, free at last of endlessly repeating his screen role. Talk about Pirandello and *Six Characters in Search of an Author* (1921)! But RKO studio officials and Gil Shepherd, the rising young actor who plays Tom Baxter (also Jeff Daniels, in a dual role), set out in search of Tom to get him back into the film and nip this terrible business of characters undertaking their own reality and walking off the screen.

Tom and Cecilia hide out in an empty amusement park. When Cecilia goes alone into a coffee shop to get them some donuts and coffee, handsome Gil Shepherd nabs her and insists she take him to see Tom. They enter a dark pavilion near the merry-go-round.

CECILIA

Tom? Tom?

TOM

Cecilia, I dreamed of us in Cairo. We . . .

CECILIA

Tom. Tom . . . eh, I-I brought, eh, I brought Gil Shepherd.

GIL

Gil, Gil Shepherd. I play you in the movie.

TOM

You do?

GIL

How dare you run away?

TOM

This is disconcerting.

GIL

Oh, I'll show you the meaning of disconcerting. I'm trying to build a career!

TOM

Yeah, well, I don't want to be in the film anymore. I'm in love with Cecilia.

CECILIA

Mr. Shepherd, you said you weren't angry.

GIL

You can't do this to me. It's my best role. I've been criti-cally acclaimed for this. It's my very—

TOM

I'd say, it's because of the way I do it.

GIL

No, no, no, because of the way I do it. I'm doing it, not you. It, it, it, it's me, not him. I mean, isn't that obvious?

TOM

Well, then, how do you explain that here I am?

GIL

Well, because I took you from the printed page, and I made you live. I fleshed you out, just like—

TOM

So, I'm living.

GIL

Yes, but for the screen only, please. And as soon—

TOM

I want my freedom.

GIL

I don't want another one of me running around the world. I mean, I can just imagine what he's been up—

TOM

Why? Are you, are you afraid I'll embarrass you?

GIL

Yes. Frankly I am afraid—

TOM

But, y-y-you created me.

GIL

All right, look—I'm, be reasonable here. I'm starting to build a career. Is life up on the screen so terrible that you—

TOM

I wanted to be with Cecilia. I'm in love with her.

GIL

Will you tell him to go back? Tell him you, tell him that you don't love him. Tell him you *can't* love him. He's fictional! You want to waste your time with a fictional character? I mean, you're a sweet girl. You deserve an actual human.

CECILIA

B-but Tom's perfect!

GIL

Yeah, uh, but he's not real. What good is "perfect" if the man's not real?

TOM

I can learn to be real. It's easy. You know, there's nothing to it. Uh, being real comes very naturally to me.

GIL

Can't learn to be real. It's like learning to be a midget. It's not a thing you can learn. Some of us are real, some are not.

TOM

I say I can do it.

GIL

I'm not going to stay here and argue with you. I'm gonna go back to town. I'm gonna call my attorney, the Actors' Union. I won't take this lying down . . . nor will Raoul Hirsch, nor the police, nor the FBI!

—*The Purple Rose of Cairo* (1985), Woody Allen

Woody Allen shores up his illusionary plot with four more Tom Baxters across the country threatening to walk off their screens and deepening the gloom of the beleaguered producer of the film within the film, Raoul Hirsch. In this scene, Cecilia remains sidelined while Tom and Gil thrash out Tom's status as a fictional reality. Aside from being a big, prickly face-off between them, the scene gives solidity to the plot, with Jeff Daniels—as Tom in pith helmet and breeches and as Gil in a gorgeous camel's hair coat—deftly playing against himself in the same frame. We actually see the film character and the actor who created him face-to-face, and Cecilia adds nothing to their drama but her helpless belief in Tom's reality. Later, Gil himself makes a play for Cecilia, who—torn between Tom and Gil—wails, "I'm confused. I . . . I'm married. I-I-I just met a wonderful new man. He's fictional, but you can't have everything." To which an annoyed Gil replies, "I'm plagued by my own creation."

At times, as in Sturges, the screen fills chockablock with strongly edged (or cast) characters, especially in the black-and-white *Purple Rose*, which rises to heights of pleasure for us when Tom pulls Cecilia back into the screen with him and Cecilia finds herself caught up in a madcap Manhattan weekend with society folk at the Copacabana and in a lavish apartment with a fashionable white phone—a bit of swank Cecilia can't believe real.

The face-off scene builds planks under Cecilia's wonder—she only reacts silently throughout. Allen's dialogue for Tom and Gil gives each character a through-line to play: Tom plays both "disconcerting" surprise at meeting his creator, Gil, and firm desire to hang on to his freedom. Gil plays ego, the self-drunken, rising young star who sees his career slipping away because of this unruly character he's created. The stuttering lines play as if improvised on the through-lines. Some writers might well be at a loss how to handle this scene, and flail away at it with feeble invention. Allen did not invent this scene a line at a time: he stood back and asked himself, What's up here?—and had well in mind Gil's emptily forceful exit calling up Raoul Hirsch and the F.B.I., threats lacking menace except in Gil's mind. But Allen, as an actor himself, knows that Jeff Daniels has to give body to both characters and so grants Daniels deeply opposing through-lines to play. The "two" actors can say nearly anything if anchored emotionally into warring characters—their feelings will carry the scene. Allen's greater problem lies in the overall structure of the script and the purposes of this scene—the lines come second and will arise from Tom being upriver of Gil in the plot. Happily for us, Allen lets these two handsome airheads clash with stronger lines than most of us could dream up, and with stage business I've not talked about. We watch this pivotal scene sharply, less for the humor assured by the freakish situation (someone playing two people in split-screen assures theatricality as handily as giving Hamlet Yorick's skull for a little chat—"Hamlet, talk to the skull for a minute!") than in fear that the plot-bubble just might burst at this "realistic" moment. But the strength of the face-off soothes our fears as does its underlying parody of movie talk ("This is disconcerting"). And, though we don't know it as we watch this scene, Cecilia's utter belief in what happens here adds to the rapture in her solo final scene as—seated alone at the Jewel, her eyes standing with water or wonder, Tom now back in his film, the *Purple Rose* pulled and replaced by *Top Hat*, and Gil having offered to take her to Hollywood and then deserted her—she watches Fred Astaire sing "Cheek to Cheek" to Ginger Rogers and the famed team dance on a liquid black floor mounted with a pure white set in blue-toned black-and-white, her eyes locking into illusion, deepening, deepening, and at last surrendering without hold to the celluloid dreamworld.

As with most of Pirandello, the script explores the nature of reality and illusion. Could *Purple Rose* have been better written? For its own purposes, the writing shines, leaving big spaces for invention by the actors, the finished film marred but fitfully by dullish nonactors in roles better played by actors. But let's set it beside two similar scenes, one by Ingmar Bergman and one by Chekhov.

Bergman's grimly realistic, black-and-white *The Seventh Seal* (1957), about a disillusioned Knight (Max von Sydow) returning from the Crusades and finding Sweden swept by plague, relieves its heavy themes with intriguing fantasy. One gray dawn by a rocky seashore, Death (Bengt Ekerot)—a figure robed in black up to his snugly framed pale face, his black eyes aglitter with merciless command and bemusement—comes for the Knight. "Wait a moment," the Knight says. "You play chess, don't you?" "Yes," Death says, "I'm quite a good chess player." And the Knight seduces Death into a game before dying. The chess game goes on while the Knight's search for final wisdom unfolds—a wisdom that would be granted him in a less strong script than Bergman's, but this script paints its images with fear and palsy and offers little relief or solace. Only crumbs.

Along the way home the Knight comes to a gray stone church and goes in. A soft noise in the confessional draws him to the grill of the booth. We see Death's face behind the grill but the Knight doesn't.

KNIGHT

I want to talk to you as openly as I can, but my heart is empty. *[Death doesn't answer.]* The emptiness is a mirror turned toward my own face. I see myself in it, and I am filled with fear and disgust. *[Death doesn't answer.]* Through my indifference to my fellow men, I have isolated myself from their company. Now I live in a world of phantoms. I am imprisoned in my dreams and fantasies.

DEATH

And yet you don't want to die.

KNIGHT

Yes, I do.

DEATH

What are you waiting for?

KNIGHT

I want knowledge.

DEATH

You want guarantees?

KNIGHT

Call it whatever you like. Is it so cruelly inconceivable to grasp God with the senses? Why should he hide himself in a mist of half-spoken promises and unseen miracles? *[Death doesn't answer.]* How can we have faith in those who believe when we can't have faith in ourselves? What is going to happen to those of us who want to believe but aren't able to? And what is to become of those who neither want to nor are capable of believing? *[Complete silence.]* Why can't I kill God within me? Why does he live on in this painful and humiliating way even though I curse Him and want to tear Him out of my heart? Why, in spite of everything, is He a baffling reality that I can't shake off? Do you hear me?

DEATH

Yes, I hear you.

KNIGHT

I want knowledge, not faith, not suppositions, but knowledge. I want God to stretch out his hand toward me, reveal Himself and speak to me.

DEATH

But he remains silent.

KNIGHT

I call out to him in the dark but no one seems to be there.

DEATH

Perhaps no one is there.

KNIGHT

Then life is an outrageous horror. No one can live in the face of death, knowing that all is nothingness.

DEATH

Most people never reflect about either death or the futility of life.

KNIGHT

But one day they will have to stand at that last moment of life and look toward the darkness.

DEATH

When *that* day comes . . .

KNIGHT

In our fear, we make an image, and that image we call God.

DEATH

You are worrying . . .

KNIGHT

Death visited me this morning. We are playing chess together. This reprieve gives me the chance to arrange an urgent matter.

DEATH

What matter is that?

KNIGHT

My life has been a futile pursuit, a wandering, a great deal of talk without meaning. I feel no bitterness or self-reproach because the lives of most people are very much like this. But I will use my reprieve for one meaningful deed.

DEATH

Is that why you are playing chess with Death?

KNIGHT

He is a clever opponent, but up to now I haven't lost a single man.

DEATH

How will you outwit Death in your game?

KNIGHT

I use a combination of the bishop and the knight which he hasn't yet discovered. In the next move I'll shatter one of his flanks.

DEATH

I'll remember that.

Death shows his face at the grill of the confession booth for a moment but disappears instantly.

—*The Seventh Seal* (1957),
Ingmar Bergman

A strong visual caps this scene as the Knight raises his hand and looks at it in the sunlight through a tiny window. "This is my hand," he says, Hamlet again with Yorick's skull. "I can move it, feel the blood pulsing through it. The sun is still high in the sky and I, Antonius Block, am playing chess with Death." And he makes a fist of his hand and lifts it to his temple in a surge of faith in himself.

Again we have a writer inspired to set a figure of fantasy beside a real person, and the Knight accepts Death as quickly as Cecilia accepts Tom stepping out of the screen. No questions. The silent writer tells us simply, You must accept this premise if we're to have a play. However, Bergman adds much more realism than Allen, with crawling lines of penitents whipping themselves, a "witch" burned alive, and everywhere the heavy depression of the age and its religion. Few viewers can part Bergman's tortured images of Christianity from those of the plague— neither really seems worse than the other, although many characters speak feelingly of God and an innocent juggler even sees Mary teaching the Christ child to walk by holding on to her fingers. Love of Christ is not absent; only God vanishes, all light abandoned.

Also, Bergman has a much stronger sense of the natural world than Allen: a squirrel runs up the stump of a just-fallen tree,* a hawk (the opening shot) hovers like the human spirit itself above a gray sea (though a bird also her-

*The squirrel is a lucky accident not in the published script, which misses many touches from the finished film. While Allen's published scripts read as if from the finished films and capture all the hesitations and stammerings, few movie scripts catch the emotion and suspense we come to love in films—the high tide of our belief as actors, makeup, costumes, script, set decoration, photography, and music support one another. For my money, even the best scripts sink under their stage and camera directions, which is why I mostly leave these pleasureless devices to your imagination herein.

alds the horrors of the Apocalypse, the Book of Revelation tells us), the Knight's face dances with light shining from a wooden bowl of milk as he gives the script's most uplifting speech while thanking the pure-innocent juggler and his wife for the milk and strawberries they set before him: "I shall remember this moment. The silence, the twilight, the bowls of strawberries and milk, your faces in the evening light . . . I'll try to remember what we have talked about. I'll carry this memory between my hands as carefully as if it were a bowl filled to the brim with fresh milk. And it will be an adequate sign—it will be enough for me." This quiet, milk-lighted speech shimmers with Shakespearean eloquence against the astral gray—it's not to be missed, friend.

Allen's realism depends on the pricking of movie conventions and on our bottomless thoughts about the life of figures on film. Can someone really be dead who acts on film? Well, are Cervantes and Shakespeare dead, who act on paper? Yes, the dead are dead, but in all art some piece of the spirit lives on, like the heady smell of life ripening in a hot field of waving wheat: it's up to us to stand in the noon sun and drink down the life-giving spirit breathed into a story by its creator. So we welcome the fantasy of a figure stepping down from a screen: it's something true we believe in quite aside from storytelling. This strange acceptance springs from psychic bedrock, the desire for bodily rebirth. We *long* to believe in it. It feeds us at the heart's core. So Allen's playful realism lifts us into accepting the Depression era in color film, with charming sets and costumes, just as strongly as Bergman's stress on physical realism plunges us into the Middle Ages. The realism in both films flows out of a yearning to place our spirit back into the Depression or the Middle Ages and test it against those times. How would we act in those days? Bergman, by the way, recalls the film chiefly for its freeing him from his fear of death—and also that it "was fun reconstructing a whole epoch with such incredibly simple means." *Fun. Play. Entertainment.* WRITING IS FUN—even if it's about the Apocalypse—OR YOU'RE DOING SOMETHING WRONG.

Okay, reading movie dialogue to ourselves, it's worse than being deaf at the opera. How can you know about the glowing planes of tall, gaunt, burning, twenty-seven-year-old Max von Sydow's face, his cropped blond hair and long, narrow, brooding skull, the through-line of tortured mental activity he plays silently, the shine of his pale blue eyes as he bares his soul in the confessional while Death's merciless charcoal eyes listen? But—one final drama, before we move on to novels and stories.

In 1895 Anton Chekhov (who broke into print as the joke-popping Woody Allen of his day), writing the first draft of his first play, *The Seagull* (in one month), told a friend: "Believe it or not, I'm writing a play. . . . I can't say I don't enjoy writing it, though I'm flagrantly disregarding the basic tenets of the stage. The comedy has three female roles, six male roles, four acts, a landscape (the view of a lake), much conversation about literature, little action, and five tons of love."

Well, won't five tons of love make good any shortcomings? Ahh, the first performance—a critical disaster on a scale with the greatest theatrical or musical disasters: Chekhov felt, he said, as if he'd been "punched in the face." Nobody had expected the adored humorist to be so lackadaisical about structure or to write a play that, as he said, begins *forte* and ends *pianissimo*. Years passed before he recovered faith in his play. What the hell, medicine's my wife, Dr. Chekhov said, literature only my mistress.

A fairly banal plot about a brilliant young actress driven mad by a respected writer holds this play together—but it's about feelings, not what happens. Many of the big moments and richest effects come in the pauses, as we experience for ourselves what a character thinks. This then-highly-original device—much like today's movies, with the actors' eyes telling us more than the lines—angered everyone. Even the actors could not grasp that they had to give up great poses and speech-making. In the scene that follows, the writer Trigorin reveals the secrets of writing to the budding young actress, Nina, Chekhov's seagull beating in heaven, and many thought this the worst scene in the play: seemingly it feeds *nothing* into the action. "Anton, Anton! My God, everything STOPS!" Of course, here Boris Alexeyevich Trigorin sinks his hook so firmly into Nina that she'll do anything for him, this being the play's strongest moment, as reader or viewer rises to his or her hottest focus and weighs every syllable.

NINA

Good morning, Boris Alexeyevich.

TRIGORIN

Good morning. It appears that something came up and we're leaving today. I'm afraid you and I may never meet again. I'm sorry. I don't often come across young women, young interesting women. My God, I've already forgotten how it feels to be eighteen or nineteen. Can't imagine it, not clearly. The young women in my stories are quite fake—not at all lifelike. Ugh, horrible. How I'd like to be in your shoes!—if only for an hour. Then I'd know what you think, ha—what manner of creature you are.

NINA

And I'd like to be in your shoes!

TRIGORIN

Why?

NINA

So I'd know how it feels to be gifted and famous. A writer! What does fame feel like? What sensation does it give you?

TRIGORIN

What sensation? None, I guess. I've never thought about it. *[Thinking]* So it must be one of two things. Either you greatly exaggerate my fame. Or fame has no sensation.

NINA

But—you read about yourself in the papers?

TRIGORIN

They praise me and I like it. Or they pan me and I'm depressed. For a day or two.

NINA

But what a world to live in! Don't you know how I envy you? Life is so different for everyone! Some people can barely drag themselves through their tiresome tiny lives. And they're all miserable. But you—you are one in a million—you are blessed. Brilliant, interesting, a life full of meaning. . . . You are happy.

TRIGORIN

Really? Hm! . . . Well, fame and happiness, my brilliant, interesting life, I see. Just pretty words? Actually, I don't like marmalade. But you are very young and kind.

You have a delightful life!

TRIGORIN

What's so good about it? *[Looking at his watch, mock-seriously]* I must get back to my writing bench. Excuse me, please, I'm obsessed. *[Laughs]* See, you've stepped on my favorite corn. And I get excited—angry—both at once. Okay, let's talk. About my ravishing and brilliant life . . . Mm. Where should I start? *[Thinking]* You *have* heard of obsessions?—where a man is haunted day and night by some idea—the moon or something? Well, I have my moon. Day and night I'm obsessed by one compulsion: Why am I not writing? I must write, I must write. Write, write, write . . . And no sooner have I written The End to one story, but the compulsion grips me again. Then I must write a third, then a fourth. I write without stopping!—except to change horses. I'm a robot, I have no choice. Now what's so damned delightful and brilliant about that? Tell me. Nina, it's a dog's life. Now, I'm sitting here talking with you, even getting a little excited—and delighted—but I can't forget for one second that I have a manuscript on my desk howling for me like a Pomeranian. A dog's life. I see a cloud shaped like a grand piano—and I beat into my forehead that I must mention somewhere in my story that a cloud flat as a grand piano passed by. I smell some heliotrope. Beat my forehead. Sickly smell, purple with mourning. Must paste on—summer evening. My net and I lie in wait for every pretty phrase that lights on my lips—or on yours— and all these pretty words get pinned to my writing cabinet *[tapping forehead]*. You darling, you may come in handy someday. I finish something?—I fly to the theater, or go fishing, I need to rest! Forget myself! Ahh, what's this?—a new subject, turning, turning. My brain's magnetized, a heavy steel ball, and an invisible force draws me to my desk. Hurry up, write! Write! And so on. Forever and ever and ever. This dog rest?—never. *And*— I'm eating myself alive. The honey I offer to the darkness comes from my most private stores. I don't want to tell these things! But I pluck out jar after jar and give it away. Boris, you're mad. Who calls me sane? "Boris, yawn, what are you writing now? Who's getting it in the back?" That's it, over and over. And I feel they're all faking me out, all their deep interest, praise, admiration— it's a lie. I live in a lie, the way you tell a sick man how well he looks—he loves it, of course—but, uh, the day will come, I know, when they sneak up behind me with a strait jacket—and it's off to the bughouse for Boris Alexeyevich. Now in my youth, the old days, mm, maybe the best days, writing was torture without end. I was unimportant, and when I lucked out, I felt clumsy, awkward, superfluous. Your nerves pull thin, you're pins and needles all over. You hang without shame around better writers and artists and people on top. Nobody knows you, at best you're a pimple—you can't look people in the eye. You're a passionate, cold-blooded gambler without a buck to get into the game. My unseen reader?—a sneaky sonofabitch, not to be trusted. The public?—I shook when I thought of it. It TERRified me! When I had a new play put on, I knew instantly that the people with dark hair in the audience were hostile—and the blonds cold. Indifferent. Their hair—frightened me! My God, what agony.

NINA

But . . . inspiration!—the process of creation!—these *must* give you sublime and happy moments.

TRIGORIN

Before they pass they do. And looking over proofs is pleasant. But as soon as a thing is published my heart sinks. The damned thing's a failure! a botch—I should never have written it. I get angry with myself—I'm just—rubbish. HA! And the public reads it and says, "Old Trigorin hasn't lost his touch, it's charming. So clever! Of course, it's not Tolstoy." Or, "A delightful story! But not up to Turgenev and *Fathers and Sons*." And so on, to my dying day. Clever and charming, clever and charming—that's it. And when I die, my friends will pass by my grave and mourn, "Here lies Trigorin. A charming writer—but not Turgenev."

NINA

Excuse me, Boris Alexeyevich. I *refuse* to understand you. *You* are spoiled by success.

TRIGORIN

What success! I've never satisfied *myself*. My dear Nina, I do not care for myself as a writer. And worse than that, I'm often bewildered and don't understand what I write. I love this lake, these trees, the sky. I have a feeling for nature. It wakes my passions—an irresistible need to write. And I spend this desire with great skill. But, my dear, I am something more than a landscape painter. I'm a citizen!—I love my country. I love its people. If I'm any kind of a writer, I must speak of the people, their suffering, their future. I must speak of science, and of the rights of man *et cetera, et cetera*. But when I speak, I'm attacked, angrily, by everyone. I race about like a fox who hears the hounds. I see life and science flying farther and farther ahead of me as I fall farther and farther back—like some man chasing a train. In the end, what I really do best, is landscape. In all else, I fake it. It's lifeless. And I'm false to the very marrow of my bones.

NINA

You work too hard. You don't have time to know how important you are—and you don't wish to. So you're dissatisfied with yourself. Other people think you're wonderful. Great! If I were a writer—if I were you—I'd recognize that I may be sacrificing my life to the millions, but I'd know that the greatest happiness of those millions is that my sacrifice raises them to my level. I'd know their happiness pulls my chariot.

TRIGORIN

My chariot—well! . . . And I'm Agamemnon?
[They both smile]

NINA

For this happiness—to be a writer or an actress—I would endure the hatred of my family. I'd scrape, I'd fight. I'd live in a garret on black bread. And I'd suffer unhappiness with my work, and admitting my imperfections would not prick my dreams. But—in return, I'd demand—glory . . . real, ringing glory. *[Covering her face]* I'm dizzy. Oof!

ARKADINA

[Off-stage from the house] Boris Alexeyevich!

TRIGORIN

She's calling me. Pack up, Boris Alexeyevich! Now . . . I don't want to go. *[Looking at the lake]* Heavenly! Just *look* at it.

NINA

You see that house and garden over there? Far over?

TRIGORIN

Yes.

NINA

That was my mother's. I was born there. I spent my whole life by this lake. I know every inlet and island.

TRIGORIN

Perfect. Delicious. *[Seeing the seagull]* What's this?

NINA

A seagull. Constantine Gavrilovich shot it.

TRIGORIN

It's so lovely. Ohh, why leave! Can you talk Madame Arkadina into staying? *[Writes in his notebook]*

NINA

[Aglow] What are you writing?

TRIGORIN

[To himself] Just making notes. Had a thought. *[Putting book away]* Maybe for a short story. A girl—something like yourself, maybe—is born and lives on the shore of a lake from childhood on. She loves lifting herself over the waters like a seagull. So happy, so free—a seagull. But a monster—well, a man—comes along—out of the blue— and sees her—and ruins her. Leaves her like this seagull. Just to amuse himself. *[Pause. Arkadina opens a window]*

ARKADINA

Where are you, Boris Alexeyevich?

TRIGORIN

Coming! *[Looking at Nina. At the window:]* What's up?

ARKADINA

We're staying.
[Exit Trigorin into house]

NINA

[Comes to the foots. Long pause. Eyes closed, then shimmering brilliantly:] It's a dream!

—*The Seagull* (1896),
Anton Chekhov,
adaptation by Donald Newlove

118

Not a bad scene, though nothing happens, with Chekhov seeing it light-struck under open sky by a heavenly lake, and Trigorin (years younger than his mistress Arkadina) a soft but aging leather glove, and Nina shining-eyed, sublimely aflow, her flesh new-made by God and strong fingers dancing with eagerness. Nina fishes for Trigorin. Trigorin's no Tolstoy, of course. Or even like a character by Tolstoy, ready to hang himself with loathing before self-sacrifice redeems him. Trigorin shrinks in spirit throughout the rest of the play, marries Nina, then after their baby dies, deserts her. A number of writers, and Chekhov himself, have been taken as the model for Trigorin. But no model's needed. Trigorin's obsessions belong to all writers. For better or worse, I did my own version of Chekhov's lines—I also make free with a few stage directions—and had much, much fun reshaping Trigorin and Nina into speakable English from a lumbering thirties translation.

For me, this is the play's pivotal scene, as well it should be in its theatrical demands. Nina's lines lose much on the page, though we sense Trigorin's feelings with ease. I think Nina, the unravished virgin, cons herself throughout that Madame Arkadina's lover has his eye on her; her idealism sings before him like a blue-eyed *Heldentenor*'s—or that of a heroine of the Moscow Art Theater. Her hopeful "It's a dream!" confirms that under the lines something happens between them.

Trigorin's confessions, real or faked? Does he think the superior, Tolstoyan honesty by which he demeans himself makes him subtly more attractive to this seagull of a girl? Hey, save me, inspire me, give me your body. After all, she does do that. Isn't he like some alcoholic pleading, "I'll swear off for you"? Or does plain, simple Boris Alexeyevich speak from the heart? This scene plays many ways. We learn that after they marry he mistreats her and demeans her desire to act. In the fourth and last act, she's bent as Ophelia and thinks she's a seagull. If he does that to her offstage between the acts, what's he doing in the scene above? Something's there but not there. How would you play it? Chekhov chooses in this scene not to point a finger at Trigorin—or Nina. Of course, we may be asking questions he never asked himself, even when revising. We may well have a clearer fix on the play today than he did while writing it.

What appeals to us in this scene, aside from the living and breathing lake setting that may first have led Chekhov to write it? Well, the confessions of a writer who seemingly has it all, then does witty self-surgery that gets rather bloody—mmm! very appealing. And Nina, radiating idealism. Rub these together. Do we get Chekhovian heartbreak? A high romance sure to fall into disrepair? Or perhaps straight-on realism? It plays all three ways, depending on the through-line you choose. Imagine Jack Nicholson reading Trigorin's confessions just as Chekhov wrote them but on all three levels at once, with the Devil foremost: "Had a thought. Maybe for a short story. A girl—something like yourself, maybe—is born and lives on the shore of a lake from childhood on. She loves lifting herself over the waters like a seagull. So happy, so free—a seagull. But a monster—well, a man—comes along—out of the blue—and sees her—and ruins her. Leaves her like this seagull. Just to amuse himself." Could be quite moving. Does this tell us something? Tells us nobody has the last word on what we write.

But—now to fiction! Where we think we have the last word—unless the scriptwriters get us.

Isaac Bashevis Singer's novel *Enemies, A Love Story* (1972) may be the masterpiece of Singer's later years. Its story-telling excels at plot, character-drawing, description, and dialogue, and its black humor runs deep. A film version produced and directed by Paul Mazursky has worthwhile acting, photography, and set design, but the strongly paced script—by him and Roger L. Simon—has no time to dig into the hero's larger problems. It strives to catch Singer's deeps and his dead-silent laugh, and here and there the actors suggest the novel's characters—Ron Silver as the hero, Herman Broder, lacks Broder's haggardness, slump, thinning hair, and poor appetite (Silver's too healthy, and Mazursky's overactive sex scenes are not found in Singer), while Anjelica Huston as Herman's wife Tamara, newly risen from the dead, reads with great bitter humor but remains beautiful throughout and fails to show Tamara's growing disarray, graying hair, and the tired yellow pouches under her eyes. The actors speak Singer but look Hollywood. The film draws more readers to Singer but also creates a mock readership that feels it need not read the book—it has seen this well-made, attractively acted movie, with its damned entertaining but hastily made plot points and dialogue skimmed from the novel.

I'll let Singer's descriptive verve lead us into his dialogue. Here, Herman takes his third wife (he has three at once and two are pregnant) to a party during a snowstorm:

> It was late when Herman and Masha stepped out of the train into the street. A wild wind was blowing from the frozen Hudson River. Masha clung to Herman. He had to lean into the wind with all his weight in order not to be blown back. Snow covered his eyelids. Masha, gasping, shouted something to him. His hat tried to tear

itself off his head. His coattails and trousers whipped about his legs. It was a miracle that they were able to make out the number on the rabbi's house. He and Masha ran breathlessly into the lobby. Here it was warm and tranquil. Gold-framed pictures hung on the walls; carpets covered the floors; chandeliers diffused soft light; sofas and easy chairs awaited the guests.

I explore this paragraph with you to show something about description as dialogue. In this flat but somehow gorgeous passage Singer talks with himself but with no outward sign of soul-searching. It shows Singer at his purest, his hallmark black humor pitting the violence of nature against the warmth of wealth (how far from Herman's wartime hideaway and Masha's camps), his vigor here as flat-out his own as Van Gogh's paste-thick strokes. What is the voice? Singer gives himself over to upwelling invention and engages in nature writing that never forgets the overarching demands of plot. Anxiety-ridden Herman and Masha face a New York blizzard that billows about them much like the horrors that nearly buried them under the Nazis. Singer's flatness allows us to supply the terrible cold blowing off the flat width of the Hudson River, the snow caking them, the sapping hardship of even moving in such deep snow against wind howling into their faces and whipping their clothes. But, of course, he knows he will deliver them by a miracle into the sudden warmth and peace of the rabbi's lobby, which somehow flows into an apartment hung with gold-framed pictures, covered with carpets, diffused with soft light from chandeliers, and where sofas and easy chairs await the guests.

Singer had as much satisfaction writing this paragraph, of plunging his hands into hot blood at his imagination's core, as Keats had writing his odes. To sit still and let the lines spurt onto the page, each line paced and shaped to his voice at its clearest, and then to give flow to the lines, let them build, add a pause or caesura at the three-quarter mark ("It was a miracle . . ."), and then to let flood the warm reversal of harsh sensations that caps the paragraph—all this binds Singer to his soul and becomes a religion stronger than the spiritual doubts besetting his characters. Singer at least can trust to a verve within. This dialogue of self and soul—a rising and diving of fragments moving forward (wild wind blowing, Masha clung, lean into, blown back, snow covered, Masha gasping, shouted, hat tearing, coattails and trousers whipping) like musical motifs between man and nature answering each other above and below the staff—is the call and response at the heart of all great fiction.

At the party, Herman's wife Masha goes berserk when she learns that a third wife, Tamara—his first wife of ten years' standing in Poland and reportedly shot to death by the Nazis—still lives. Now in 1949 and carrying a bullet in her hip, Tamara comes to New York, Herman not only having remarried but married his pregnant Masha as well. A lost philosopher who does not believe in God, Herman grubs for life as a ghostwriter for a rabbi become rich and famous both on Herman's work and his own chutzpah. Spiritual laws from rival rabbis forever crisscross and cancel each other out in Herman's mind but become the manure of his ghostwritings. Somewhere in the real world of Coney Island, the Bronx, and the subway wastes under Manhattan, Herman still hides out from the Nazis, as he did for three years in a hayloft in Poland. The movie's Herman gives off more life and ease with his new American society than does Singer's Herman, a bony, driven wreck with no bodily beauty. He is the Jewish life force down to its last flame and kept alive by women. A ghost, he barters his flame to pay the rent on two apartments and feed two households, with his ghostwife—their ten-year marriage and dead children still clinging to her—now joining him from the beyond.

In this scene, after a wealthy realtor named Pesheles unwittingly reveals to wife Masha that wife Tamara's alive in New York, Herman the hired ghost rushes unfed from his employer's fabulous party back into the blizzard and finds refuge in a Broadway cafeteria, soon to close at 2:00 A.M. He phones Tamara in Manhattan, who's just come from the hospital, her hip bullet now removed.

"I hope I didn't wake you. It's me, Herman."

"Yes, Herman."

"Were you asleep?"

"No, I was reading the newspaper."

"Tamara, I'm in a cafeteria on Broadway. They close at two o'clock. I have nowhere to go."

Tamara hesitated a moment. "Where are your wives?"

"They're both not speaking to me."

"What are you doing on Broadway at this hour?"

"I was at a party at the rabbi's."

"I see. Would you like to come here? It's bitter cold. I've pulled the sleeves of a sweater over my legs. There's a wind whistling through the house as if there wasn't a pane in the windows. Why are your wives fighting with you? On second thought, why don't you come right over? I was thinking of calling you tomorrow. There's something I have to talk to you about. The only problem is that they lock the outside door. You can ring the bell for two hours and the janitor won't come to open it.

When will you be here? I'll go down and open it myself."

"Tamara, I'm ashamed to be bothering you like this. It's just that I've no place to sleep and don't have the money to pay for a hotel."

"Now, when she's pregnant, she's started a campaign against you?"

"She's being egged on from all sides. I don't want to blame you, but why did you have to tell Pesheles about me?"

Tamara sighed. "He came to the hospital and descended on me with a thousand questions. I still can't figure out how he got there. He sat down next to my bed and cross-examined me like a prosecutor. He tried to make a match for me too. It was soon after the operation. What kind of people are these?"

"I've got myself into such a mess that everything is hopeless," Herman said. "I'd better go back to Coney Island."

"At this hour? It will take you all night. No, Herman, come to my place. I can't sleep. I'm up all night anyway."

—*Enemies, A Love Story* (1972),
Isaac Bashevis Singer

This dialogue feeds on facts, the stripped and hopeless Now. Herman sees no way out—of his wives, the blizzard, the rabbi's grip on his ghost. Only Tamara offers some kind of philosophical overview ("What kind of people are these?"), but that's not much. The real reason for this scene's existence lies in Singer wishing to move Herman into Tamara's influence and bedevil him even more. The title *Enemies* covers not just a love story but also Herman's universe of enemies, from before the Nazis, through the

Nazis, into the Now: everyone he meets wishes to enslave him in some way. Slavery and enemies reach down to one-celled life, upward through the animal orders, and include his second wife Yadwiga's caged parakeets. All life turns to slavery and enemies, not to say murder, cannibalism, and worse. No words can hold back his hopelessness as Herman sits past midnight in a half-deserted cafeteria in a blizzard.

This dialogue may not seem brilliant. But part of its success lies in what's not said. Both Herman and Tamara always meet every horror with a philosophical aside. At this point, no aside helps. Herman bleeds on the rocks. Wife to writer, ghost talks to ghost. How will Singer at last get Herman into Tamara's bed? The wives who won't speak to him, the blizzard, the cafeteria's closing, the janitor who won't answer the door, the wind whistling through her apartment as if the windows have no panes, the sweater sleeves she wears on her legs, even coming downstairs after her hip operation to wait for him. All these will slip Herman into Tamara's arms for warmth, a move earned and built by Singer on hard facts chiseled from life. No call of the flesh, the novel amazes throughout by its turnings on fact and Singer's refusal to tease with sex fantasy. Even Herman's obsession with Masha rises above sex. "I can't live without her," he tells Tamara. And in Tamara's case, during their ten years apart and despite all she lived through in the Nazi work camps and as a prisoner in Russia, she remained faithful to Herman and has had no sex. "Love is no sport for me," Tamara says. Singer offers no easy lay. A small hammer blow at a time, he breaks rock for his plot, the happiest of slaves to his writing pleasures.

Let's look at an Ayn Rand kind of love scene from *The Fountainhead* (1943). Dominique Francon, a wealthy socialite, dabbles in reporting. She writes the "Your House" column that backhands slumfolk as often as their landlords, and offers criticism of architecture. Now a virgin of twenty-five, she must be dominated completely if she's ever to have sex. "I'm one of those freaks you hear about, an utterly frigid woman," she tells a would-be lover. She meets her match in Howard Roark, an architect of granite ego, who loves/rapes her without a trace of tenderness, then leaves her, wordlessly, and doesn't see her again for years. A loner who despises mass thought and turns his back on any suggestion of change in his ideas, he puts up The Enright Building, whose originality leaves him mocked by all—except Dominique. She visits him without warning one evening after her column has destroyed his chances for a new commission.

He asked: "What do you want?"

She answered: "You know what I want," her voice heavy and flat.

"Yes. But I want to hear you say it. All of it."

"If you wish." Her voice had the sound of efficiency, obeying an order with metallic precision. "I want to sleep with you. Now, tonight, and at any time you may care to call me. I want your naked body, your skin, your mouth, your hands. I want you—like this—not hysterical with desire—but coldly and consciously—without dignity and without regrets—I want you—I have no self-respect to bargain with and divide me—I want you—I want you like an animal, or a cat on a fence, or a whore."

She spoke on a single, level tone, as if she were reciting an austere catechism of faith. She stood without moving, her feet in flat shoes planted apart, her shoulders thrown back, her arms hanging straight at her sides. She looked impersonal, untouched by the words she pronounced, chaste like a young boy.

"You know that I hate you, Roark. I hate you for what

you are, for wanting you, for having to want you. I'm going to fight you—and I'm going to destroy you—and I tell you this as calmly as I told you that I'm a begging animal. I'm going to pray that you can't be destroyed—I tell you this, too—even though I believe in nothing and have nothing to pray to. But I will fight to block every step you take. I will fight to tear every chance you want away from you. I will hurt you through the only thing that can hurt you—through your work. I will fight to starve you, to strangle you on the things you won't be able to reach. I have done it to you today—and that is why I shall sleep with you tonight."

He sat deep in his chair, stretched out, his body relaxed, and taut in relaxation, a stillness being filled slowly with the violence of future motion.

"I have hurt you today. I'll do it again. I'll come to you whenever I have beaten you—whenever I know that I have hurt you—and I'll let you own me. I want to be owned, not by a lover, but by an adversary who will destroy my victory over him, not with honorable blows, but with the touch of his body on mine. That is what I want of you, Roark. That is what I am. You wanted to hear it all. You've heard it. What do you say now?"

"Take your clothes off."

—*The Fountainhead* (1943),
Ayn Rand

Dialogue of the self and soul? What else! Rand dramatizes an ethical thesis that means everything to *her*, not just to Howard and Dominique—but her manner of doing it seems forced. Dominique wants brain sex, sex of the will and reason, with sensuality a gherkin on the side. She fears that sex—an irresistible fact—may destroy her individuality and leave her faceless, a member of the masses. Roark's individualism alone can match hers and she knows that neither of them can surrender to the other without cracks shooting through their ideal selves if any tenderness or weakness shows itself. So if they have sex, they must butt together lovelessly, coldly, consciously, efficiently, with metallic precision—"not hysterical with desire" but as adversaries, leaving her austere, untouched, impersonal, "chaste like a young boy."

Howard and Dominique's idealism (or maybe just their sex lives) brought Rand millions of readers and her "Selfishness" thousands of followers. In these lovers, Rand rises above her life in Russia after the Revolution by replacing the Communism that meant to dull her spirit with mass culture, with the philosophy of a noble reverence for Self, called Objectivism. Her dialogue here—and in the movie version, which she scripted and whose lines sound utterly her own—means to be as unnatural as it reads: Rand hated Naturalism and the sorry writing and publishing of novels as if they were meant to fade as fast as magazines. She thought real-life dialogue a dead end. Since *The Fountainhead* has not been out of print in fifty years, she may have something to say about dialogue worth hearing. Is she a nut? Who cares.

In writing her film script Rand makes sure to use many of her novel's best lines, while the cast gives strong readings to extremely unnatural phrasings that barely suggest human speech. Small talk never takes place. Everyone speaks from a philosophic stance. Oddly enough, the usually shy Gary Cooper—who looks his part here—reads Roark with thought and some power (though he waffles his huge courtroom monologue), while Patricia Neal troops through Dominique's impossible lines glowingly. The picture's best lines come near the end when the villain (Robert Douglas), a vile architectural critic who undermines Roark's career, asks him, "Why don't you tell me what you think of me?" Roark's answer, "But I don't think of you," spoken as an absolute fact, shocks us. This moral superman does not give the villain even a passing thought!

Among American writers Rand should not be punished as one who sticks abstractions into her characters' mouths. Nearly all the dialogue in Melville's *Moby-Dick*, pitched at a mock-Shakespearean level that sounds like figures speaking through mouths full of fruitcake, remains in its way as false to human speech as *The Fountainhead*'s. Melville's ideas may be rich or simply as abstract as Rand's, but the dialogue in which he embeds them never breathes with life. In the excerpt above, Howard and Dominique come a hairline closer to human speech than do Ishmael and Ahab and Starbuck and the whale men of *The Pequod*. Not that human speech interests Rand, except when drawing dreary or stupid underlings who crawl through the basements of *The Fountainhead*.

Rather movingly, Rand tells us in her introduction to the novel's twenty-fifth-anniversary edition that all youths begin as Objectivists, with a noble reverence for Self, though in adults "it is virtually nonexistent. . . . This is the view with which—in various degrees of longing, wistfulness, passion and agonized confusion—the best of mankind's youth start out in life. It is not even a view, for most of them, but a foggy, groping, undefined sense made of raw pain and incommunicable happiness. It is a sense of enormous expectation, the sense that one's life is important, that great achievements are within one's capacity, and that great things lie ahead." When you think of Howard and Dominique in that light, as unstainable and unyielding adolescent gods in a filthy adult world, their dialogue becomes weirdly reasonable. Nobody starts out, Rand says, by giving up.

I've long thought *The Fountainhead* a pile of the sorriest writing ever to find popular favor, among many such doorstopper piles. Rand gives her lesser characters and dreadful straw figures thuggish dialogue and her chief villain some lifeless, all-leveling humanist rant—but I think you should stand up for your bad guys. Today I see Rand writing *The Fountainhead* in the high tide of her beliefs and feelings as a writer, a state I enjoy sharing and that gives me life when I find it welling up in others. I admire her act of creation and the thrill of achievement the finished work gave her. Remember, *Moby-Dick* sold about three thousand copies in its first seventy years, and that after his death Mozart's many piano concertos went unplayed for one hundred and fifty years, and that Beethoven's late quartets were thought too strange and intellectual for public performance for over a century after his death. The time may come, for better or worse, when the art of *The Fountainhead*, numbingly strained as it seems today, spreads its roots through an even bigger, more welcoming audience that idolizes the novel of reason and Self.

My favorite exchange in *Moby-Dick* takes place between Captain Ahab and first mate Starbuck, on deck, as Ahab enlists the crew in the search for the white whale that took his leg. The crew cries, "Aye, aye!" and Ahab is pleased.

"God bless ye," he seemed to half sob and half shout. "God bless ye, men. Steward! go draw the great measure of grog. But what's this long face about, Mr. Starbuck; wilt thou not chase the white whale? art not game for Moby Dick?"

"I am game for his crooked jaw, and for the jaws of Death too, Captain Ahab, if it fairly comes in the way of the business we follow; but I came here to hunt whales, not my commander's vengeance. How many barrels will thy vengeance yield thee even if thou gettest it, Captain Ahab? it will not fetch thee much in our Nantucket market."

"Nantucket market! Hoot! But come closer, Starbuck; thou requirest a little lower layer. If money's to be the measurer, man, and the accountants have computed their great counting-house the globe, by girdling it with guineas, one to every three parts of an inch; then, let me tell thee, that my vengeance will fetch a great premium *here!*"

"He smites his chest," whispered Stubb, "what's that for? Methinks it rings most vast, but hollow."

"Vengeance on a dumb brute!" cried Starbuck, "that simply smote thee from blindest instinct! Madness! To be enraged with a dumb thing, Captain Ahab, seems blasphemous."

"Hark ye yet again,—the little lower layer. All visible objects, man, are but as pasteboard masks. But in each event—in the living act, the undoubted deed—there, some unknown but still reasoning thing puts forth the moulding of its features from behind the unreasoning mask. If man will strike, strike through the mask! How can the prisoner reach outside except by thrusting through the wall? To me, the white whale is that wall, shoved near to me. Sometimes I think there's naught beyond. But 'tis enough. He tasks me; he heaps me; I see in him outrageous strength, with an inscrutable malice sinewing it. That inscrutable thing is chiefly what I hate; and be the white whale agent, or be the white whale principal, I will wreak that hate upon him. Talk not to me of blasphemy, man; I'd strike the sun if it insulted me. For could the sun do that, then could I do the other; since there is ever a sort of fair play herein, jealousy presiding over all creations. But not my master, man, is even that fair play. Who's over me? Truth hath no confines . . . [And much more.]"

"God keep me!—keep us all!" murmured Starbuck, lowly.

—*Moby-Dick* (1851),
Herman Melville

Now, Don, why did you cut off Ahab midspeech? Because he'd finished with the large philosophical intent of the speech and the rest is brandy and rant.

Moby-Dick swims in brandy. It's not always in focus and Melville does run on. The action scenes, though, and The Three-Day Chase—superb! I talk about *Moby-Dick* in *First Paragraphs* and *Painted Paragraphs*, the first two books in this series, and won't repeat myself here. Melville's dialogue interests me now—it's dumbfounding how poorly it sounds like speech and yet asks such rich, mindbeggaring questions. The storyteller (the sour, blackminded schoolteacher Ishmael) feels he must distance himself from the scene by feeding us information through mock-theatrical effects and stagy dialogue, as if imitation of Elizabethan playwriting will ensure long life to his page. Well, Ishmael, think ye *Moby-Dick*'s long life springs from its sorry dialogue? Nay, man, it doth not.

John Huston and Ray Bradbury got together to do the script for Huston's movie of *Moby-Dick* and moved the above sunlit scene into Ahab's shadowy cabin for the philosophical deeps of Ahab's and Starbuck's talk, a darkness which frames Ahab's obsession and brings a tight, burning-eyed focus to his great speech. Ahab shows Starbuck the charts by which they will catch the white whale. Starbuck turns to leave:

AHAB

Mr. Starbuck?

STARBUCK

I must give the helmsman our course.

AHAB

Come about, sir. Why are you wearing that long face? Are you not game for Moby Dick?

STARBUCK

Captain Ahab, I am game for any kind of death, if it comes in the way of the business we follow, that be known. But I came here to hunt whales, not my commander's vengeance. How many barrels of sperm oil will thy vengeance yield? What will it fetch on the New Bedford market?

AHAB

Money is not the measure, man. It will fetch me a great premium [striking breast] here.

STARBUCK

To be enraged with a dumb brute that struck thee out of instinct is blasphemous.

AHAB

Speak not to me of blasphemy, man. I'd strike the sun if it insulted me. Look you, Starbuck. All visible things are but as pasteboard masks. Some inscrutable yet reasoning thing puts forth the moulding of their features. The white whale tasks me. He *heaps* me. Yet he is but a mask. It is the thing behind the mask I chiefly hate, the malignant thing that has plagued and frightened man since time began, the thing that mauls and mutilates our race,

134

not killing us outright but letting us live on half a heart
and half a lung.

STARBUCK
God keep us. God keep us all. *[Exit]*

—*Moby-Dick* (1956),
script by Ray Bradbury and John Huston

Short and sweet. The inspired scriptwriters save all the
choice morsels, get in the full flavor and intent of Ahab's
madness, and vet the fake turns of speech and maunder-
ings (". . . since there is ever a sort of fair play herein, jealousy presiding over all creations. But not my master, man,
is even that fair play. Who's over me? Truth hath no confines"). They also move important adjectives (*inscrutable*
and *malignant*) to places where they work more strongly.
For me, much of *Moby-Dick* raises its sheets in the blurred
resplendencies and hifalutin ramblings of the opiated,
alcohol-laced cough syrups commonly used back then to
relieve tobacco throat, colds, sniffles, and female problems.
Melville's letters during the eighteen months of writing the
novel, during his very early thirties, mention his bad nerves
and poor sleep. Even long hours of writing need not bring
on these effects. I think Shakespeare writing *Hamlet*, his
longest, darkest graveyard play, wrote with smiling good
spirits, self-approval, a full sense of his inspired level of
imagination—and he probably slept well whatever hours
he slept. How else could he write his perhaps thirty-six
plays, the sonnets, *The Rape of Lucrece*, and whatever else he
wrote in his brief eighteen-year writing career, while carrying on a fairly heavy business life co-managing the Globe,
before retiring at forty-six? Of course, Melville came up
with the drama here between Ahab and Starbuck (its

power lessens by being on deck in broad daylight and by Ahab trying to tell all the hands as well as Starbuck about the malignant and inscrutable evil behind the whale and by then running on into mere blather) and came up with the marvelous image of the pasteboard mask and the malignancy that uses the white whale as its agent—don't think I knock his huge grip on the English tongue when it works for him. I dig the white whale's inscrutable malignancy.

Alice Hoffman's dialogue in *Seventh Heaven* falls into what Ayn Rand calls real-life dialogue and her novel into journalistic fiction about the random trivia of the day—this despite the novel's whacks at magic realism and an overriding romantic vision. Like Gabriel García Márquez's *One Hundred Years of Solitude* (1967), *Seventh Heaven* takes a set-apart, ideal community and watches it crumble in one year—not García Márquez's hundred. And without García Márquez's earlier example, Hoffman's touches of the supernatural in her Long Island suburb—a dead girl's ghost and her red high heels that walk by themselves—would be unlikely inspirations. Where García Márquez embeds his magical happenings in one long song of a novel whose sudden leaps into the unreal fit the lift of its style, Hoffman strives for a less exalted tone and so her magic takes on a secondhand clunkiness—though maybe it's just me. Nor could her storyteller's large homey voice be likely without the small-town sounds falling earthward from the heaven of Thornton Wilder's 1938 play, *Our Town*.

Hoffman's year—1959—turns the fifties decade into the sixties as all the concrete Eisenhower values fall into dust. A sexy divorced woman moving into the six-year-old neighborhood, whose brand-new houses all look alike, becomes the agent of change whose drop of color darkens (or frees) this Seventh Heaven of neighbors who all do the same thing on the same day. In this subdivision, "husbands pulled into the wrong driveways after work; children wandered into the wrong houses for cookies and milk; young mothers who took their babies out for walks in their new carriages found themselves wandering past identical houses, on identical streets, lost until twilight. . . ." A wonderful opening—one wishes Hoffman well as her imagination begins building something new out of this stiffly bound folk.

Prompted by Nora Silk, the divorced mother whose ways break the mind-set of the wives about her on Hemlock Street, Donna Durgin takes off a ton of fat with Metrecal and grapefruit, walks out of her house one evening, leaving her boorish husband and kids, and never comes back. Many months later her old married neighbor Detective Joe Hennessy (who loves Nora Silk) finds Donna selling lingerie at Lord & Taylor's fancy department store—now thin and dizzyingly beautiful. He follows her into a restaurant on her lunch break and takes her aside for a talk.

"People have been worried about you," Hennessy said. "I mean, Christ, Donna, what happened?"

"I can't explain it."

"Well, look," Hennessy said patiently, "a woman doesn't just get up one day and decide, What the hell, today I'm leaving my husband and my kids and my house and I'm not saying a damned word to anyone. You obviously knew what you were doing. No one forced you, right?"

"You wouldn't understand," Donna said.

"Well, Christ, Donna, try me!" Hennessy said. Donna looked down at the table and bit her lip and he knew she was weakening. "Just try me." Hennessy reached into the Lord & Taylor bag and brought out the black slip. "I mean, for God's sake, I already spent eighteen twenty-five on a slip."

Donna laughed in spite of herself. When the waitress came over, Hennessy ordered black coffee. As he turned back to Donna he noticed that her nails were pink and that she wore a silver bangle bracelet.

"No wedding ring," Hennessy said.

"You wouldn't understand," Donna said. "I was dead."

"What about your kids? You haven't even asked about them."

"What good was I to them?" Donna asked. "I was disappearing more each day. Is that what life is supposed to be?"

Hennessy looked at her blankly.

"Is it?" Donna asked.

"I guess it is," Hennessy said. "That's the way life is."

"Not for me," Donna said. "Not now."

Hennessy's coffee came, and when the waitress had left he leaned forward. "How would it be if everyone walked away? How would it be if I just up and left Ellen and the kids and the mortgage and just took off?"

"I don't know. How would it be?"

"God," Hennessy said. "I wish I knew."

They stared at each other and then Donna said suddenly, "I will have that coffee."

"Good. I hate to drink poison alone."

—*Seventh Heaven* (1990),
Alice Hoffman

Something really happens here in the novel's most intense and—aside from a talk between Nora and Donna at a supermarket checkout counter—second longest passage of dialogue. Hoffman's characters, perhaps because of the dreamy winter mist surrounding their homes, rarely work up much heat. Her people withdraw and keep to their ruts. Violent moments arise, echo briefly, then fade. But certain brittle character traits soften. The high school's smartest student starts hiding in pot smoke. His businessman dad leaves the family and divorces the mother. A rowdy teenage thief gives up his criminal freedom and becomes a robot citizen. Joe Hennessy's frigid wife turns to perfume and bed tricks. But Hoffman tells most of her story herself, not with her characters' dialogue. As with García Márquez, this allows for fancier writing, a more literary page unwatered by human speech.

What happens above? Detective Hennessy meets the cracks in his little civilization's walls. Hennessy has none of the cynicism mouthed by detectives in cop stories. What's it all about, Donna? he's asking. Try me! Seemingly, the mystery of Donna's disappearance would fill their talk, but the dialogue actually turns on Hennessy's baffled truth-digging and his feelings. He finds out more about himself than about Donna and now sees himself, a man of the law, as the prisoner and the woman who deserted her family the free man. A bitter drink and, like his black coffee, poison.

The same awakening becomes the through-line of the dialogue between Nora and Donna in their earlier talk at the checkout counter. Donna's awakening by Nora drives her to tears, though with the rather unconvincing detail that "her tears filled up the top of a sour cream container, then sloshed over onto the floor"—an overflowing of García Márquez, which for me violated the novel's original energies until I was drawn back in. Hoffman's magic realism misses for me in that it springs from a literary source rather than from her deepest feelings for her characters. Each magic moment rings hollow. I enjoy the art of this novel, and Nora captures me, but—unlike *Our Town* and *One Hundred Years of Solitude*—its vision does not leave me feeling enlarged. That's just me; most readers and reviewers think otherwise.

Anne Tyler's romantic drama *The Accidental Tourist* follows in the path of many of her earlier works, with a conservative Baltimore hero wrapped tight with caution. Travel writer Macon Leary lives in a psychic cocoon: his twelve-year-old son, Ethan—murdered at summer camp during a holdup at a Burger Bonanza—died a year before the story starts. In Spain, as Macon rewrites a new edition of one of his Accidental Tourist travel guides, Sarah, his wife of twenty years, decides to leave him and start fresh. A completely muffled man, Macon has problems, never acts for himself, and answers to human nature only when forced. His whole family's like this. His two brothers and sister Rose all live together in the family manse in Baltimore, and after he breaks his leg Macon moves back in with them. The three brothers and Rose share a blindness: they have no sense of left and right, tend to get lost if they walk out the front door, and can't find their way home on their own block. They arrange their many shelves of household wares and canned foods alphabetically, allspice next to ant poison. Amusing, yes, but with little sense of satire. The humor arises from the family's shared traits and the invasion of Macon's fenced-in feelings by a frizzy-headed child-woman who in no way suits him—except that she bursts his wired stuffiness like tin snips.

In this excerpt, Macon's jaunty young publisher, Julian, has been invited to the Learys' Thanksgiving dinner. He loves Rose, who is slightly older, but has never spoken a romantic word to her or of his feelings to anyone. Rose cooks the turkey a new, energy-saving way, slowly at 140 degrees, overnight, raising the temperature very high at the end of the cooking time. But her brothers see the turkey as a lump of salmonella and its stuffing as "two quarts of teeming, swarming bacteria." Rose brings in the turkey but Macon warns their guests to fill up on vegetables.

"Oh, Macon, how could you do this?" Rose asked. "My lovely turkey! All that work!"

"I think it looks delicious," Julian said.

"Yes," Porter [*Macon's elder, divorced brother*] told him, "but you don't know about the other times."

"Other times?"

"Those were just bad luck," Rose said.

"Why, of course!" Porter said. "Or economy. You don't like to throw things away; I can understand that! Pork that's been sitting too long, or chicken salad left out all night . . ."

Rose sat down. Tears were glazing her eyes. "Oh," she said, "you're all so mean! You don't fool me for an instant; I know why you're doing this. You want to make me look bad in front of Julian."

"Julian?"

Julian seemed distressed. He took a handkerchief from his breast pocket but then went on holding it.

"You want to drive him off! You three wasted your chances and now you want me to waste mine, but I won't do it. I can see what's what! Just listen to any song on the radio; look at any soap opera. *Love* is what it's all about. On soap operas everything revolves around love. A new person comes to town and right away the question is, who's he going to love? Who's going to love him back? Who'll lose her mind with jealousy? Who's going to ruin her life? And you want to make me miss it!"

"Well, goodness," Macon said, trying to sort this out.

"You know perfectly well there's nothing wrong with

that turkey. You just don't want me to stop cooking for you and taking care of this house, you don't want Julian to fall in love with me."

"Do what?"

But she scraped her chair back and ran from the room. Julian sat there with his mouth open.

"Don't you dare laugh," Macon told him.

Julian just went on gaping.

"Don't even consider it."

Julian swallowed. He said, "Do you think I ought to go after her?"

"No," Macon said.

"But she seems so—"

"She's fine! She's perfectly fine."

"Oh."

"Now, who wants a baked potato?"

There was a kind of murmur around the table; everyone looked unhappy. "That poor, dear girl," Mrs. Barrett said. "I feel just awful."

"Me too," Susan said.

"Julian?" Macon asked, clanging a spoon. "Potato?"

"I'll take the turkey," Julian said firmly.

At that moment, Macon almost liked the man.

—*The Accidental Tourist* (1985),
Anne Tyler

Moving, wonderfully amusing, and yet anchored in character. Sooner or later, every writer faces a dinner scene—or at least a four-handed card game—whose first draft comes less easily than sledging smiles into boulders. You chisel off "he saids" and "she saids," scrape away feelingful adverbs, and sink the feelings back into the speech itself. Instead of " 'I'm such a schmuck,' I said, ruefully," you write, "I'm such a schmuck." It's all there. Instead of " 'Julian?' Macon asked, to change the subject. 'Potato?,' " you write, " 'Julian?' Macon asked, clanging a spoon. 'Potato?' " The leap from "to change the subject" to "clanging a spoon" may not come until the third draft. When it does, though, angels chime softly in your head, *"CHMmm-mmm!"* Great fun, these sweaty scenes, like beating your dull twin at handball.

To pull from a fine novel a brilliant script whose colors suggest the original calls for a different joy. Director-scriptwriter Lawrence Kasdan and his cowriter, Frank Galati, seamlessly join pieces of stained glass from all over the novel into strips of film bright with Tyler dialogue and description. The Thanksgiving turkey scene sticks to the novel, but drops Porter's children and trims and sharpens the original, knowing that here less is more: the actors will supply a solidity of story and sense of human presence spelled out by the novel but taken for granted by the scriptwriters for whom the very *ongoingness* of film moves the story unstoppably while costumed actors in makeup give presence simply by being there.

ROSE

Macon! how could you do this? My lovely turkey, all that work!

JULIAN

I think it looks delicious.

PORTER

Yes, but you don't know about the other times.

JULIAN

Other times?

ROSE

You don't fool me for an instant. You want me to look bad in front of Julian. You want to drive him off. You three wasted your chances and now you want me to waste mine. But I won't do it. I can see what's what. Love is what it's all about—you want to make me miss it.

MACON

Well, goodness.

ROSE

You just don't want me to stop cooking for you and taking care of this house. You don't want Julian to fall in love with me.

MACON

Do what? *[Exit Rose]*

JULIAN

Do you think I ought to go after her?

MACON

No.

MRS. BARRETT

That poor, dear girl. I feel just awful.

JULIAN

But she seems so—

MACON

She's fine. She's perfectly fine. Now who wants a baked potato?—Julian, potato?

JULIAN

I'll take the turkey. *[Cutting firmly into bird]*

—*The Accidental Tourist* (1988),
script by Lawrence Kasdan and Frank Galati

William Hurt plays Macon, Bill Pullman Julian, Amy Wright Rose, David Ogden Stiers Porter, and Peggy Converse Mrs. Barrett, with Hurt giving his finest work ever and Tyler, Kasdan, and Galati offering him in every frame much to fill out. The scriptwriters trim away Porter's talk about Rose's bacterial pork and chicken salad, and lop a chunk from Rose's delightfully screwy monologue about love in the soaps and replace it quite simply with "Love is what it's all about"—which works. And out goes Macon's "Don't you dare laugh . . . Don't you even consider it" to Julian. Julian's too amazed to laugh, heaven having dropped into his lap, though Macon fails to grasp this. All told, Tyler should have no gripes about this scene and how it plays.

Are we accidental tourists, in love with our home hearths, but battered by casual evil? Sarah remains still in the grip of this thought, while Macon has his frizzy-headed girlfriend with her pan-allergic child as his life preservers. He at last makes a decision for himself rather than fall passively before random forces. Is that the best we can do, strike out for the life preserver as the sea lifts and drops us? Just having another human being to hold on to gives us spirit. But we also have Macon's recourse to maxims, for ourselves and other hearth-loving tourists, to warn or at least prepare us for what Macon calls (his murdered son in mind) "devastating losses." Warnings may not be much, but they add to our strength, preparedness being half the battle, whatever our losses. Hoffman may try for a more scenic page and strike for bolder stylistic effects than Tyler, but Tyler's characters cast a more rounded image onto our minds and act more richly, with deeper consequences to their actions. And Tyler rakes around more tirelessly in the human spirit to find what she can among the rocks. Am I lordly? Do I puff Tyler at Hoffman's expense? Well, Tyler's a generation older and *The Accidental Tourist* engages me as wiser than *Seventh Heaven*.

The strongest scene in Terry McMillan's second novel, *Disappearing Acts*, also happens to be a Thanksgiving dinner. In this story, Zora Banks, a twenty-nine-year-old black schoolteacher who wants to be a singer-composer, moves into a new flat in Brooklyn, where she falls for a handsome construction worker, Franklin Swift, a man built like a linebacker but with a certain psychological problem. Raised by a "bitch" mother and "chump" father, Franklin has been trained to fail by Moms, as have her other children. Whenever Franklin gets laid off or slips between jobs, his powerful self-regard caves in, he falls into the very limbo his mother said he'd be in, and he vents his fears and low self-esteem on his women—a piece of his character Zora knows nothing about. Midway through the novel, fearfully, he takes Zora home to meet his family for Thanksgiving dinner. She spends eighty dollars and seven hours having her hair set in cornrows. Zora withholds from Franklin that she began having epileptic fits at twelve—but has had none in four years. Because of these, she doesn't drink alcohol—but at dinner a stiff drink lands before her, which she finishes, and during dinner Zora talks about the need for blacks to have individual "master plans" for their lives. Blacks can't go on blaming white folks for *everything*, she insists, adding that the reason some blacks fail in life goes back to their parents. Moms's lips curl down. Franklin tells us:

> My Moms jabbed her fork against her plate, and it made a scraping noise. She just looked at Zora, then shoved some food in her mouth. She looked like she was getting ready to say something but was too damn mad to say it. The real deal was that Zora just struck a damn chord.

"Meaning what?" I asked.

"Meaning if they instilled more confidence in us, maybe we'd grow up feeling more secure about who we are and what we're capable of doing, that's all."

Just then my Moms threw her fork down on the table, jumped up, and said, "Why don't you just shut up!" She dug her fingers in her plate and threw some mashed potatoes in Zora's face.

Everybody—including me—lunged up, then stood around the table staring at my Moms like she was crazy. I swear I saw silver stars dancing in fronta my eyes, so I blinked hard a few times, then realized this shit was happening for real. Zora was backing her chair away from the table, looking like she was in shock. I didn't even realize I was walking in my Moms' direction, with my fist balled up. But Pops grabbed my arm.

"Son, please," he said. Then he turned to Moms. "Jerry! You just had to do something ignorant, didn't you? You just couldn't be satisfied until you spoiled everything, could you? Who in the hell do you think you are, pulling some stupid-ass shit like this? Damn." He threw his napkin on the table and stood up. Pops was fuming—his nostrils was flared—and he was licking his lips like he was getting ready to spit on her or something. I ain't seen him this mad in years. He was looking down at her like she was a dog that just bit him and he was trying to decide if he should kick it.

I couldn't believe he had just talked to her like that, even though this ain't the first time she done pulled some rank shit like this.

"The girl talks too damn much. Just like the rest of them sluts Franklin done brought home, trying to get my approval. They all the same, except this one done been to college and think she know everything. Well, not in my book. And I ain't gotta sit in my own house listening to what she thinks is wrong with black folks 'cause she think she so damn high-and-mighty."

—*Disappearing Acts* (1989),
Terry McMillan

And Moms goes right on eating her Thanksgiving meal, alone, while her two daughters jump all over her, then serves herself a big piece of sweet potato pie.

McMillan's brilliant main theme in her novel lies in how people disappear into themselves, either as a retreat from what they see as flaws in their characters or as a way of becoming safe from attack. *Disappearing Acts* is not about blacks abandoning their families, although Franklin opts out from life with his sharp-toothed, three-hundred-pound first wife and their likable children. Franklin quit school after eleventh grade, so he writes in black English, while the chapters Zora tells show polish even as she and her three girlfriends trade colorful pussy talk and chat about dicks. The reader well hooked, the sex talk dims.

Franklin's description of the Thanksgiving dinner talks to the readers as if dialogue. His sentences zing if trimmed, but would they be stronger? What if Franklin gave up the passive voice—"Zora was backing her chair away from the table, looking like she was in shock"—and voiced this sentence actively: "Zora backed her chair from the table, shocked"? Here the passive voice, with some art, imitates Franklin's shock. His character's not keyed to a hip style and so McMillan chooses to stay within Franklin's voice and not grant him livelier word sense—though he *has* read *Webster's Dictionary* and always beats Zora at Scrabble.

Many good things happen in this passage: the worm turns as pussywhipped Pops attacks Moms. And McMillan draws Moms skillfully, finding the novel's most original scene in Moms's nutty indifference to her mistreatment of a dinner guest, which works not just because Moms acts out her spitefulness, and her madness, but also because each person at table reacts strongly in character—a hard trick to pull off. This scene both wrote itself and, I'm sure, demanded intense thought—and I'll bet McMillan slapped her desk with joy when Moms hurled the spuds. She later caps this scene with the dizzied and suddenly drunk Zora in Franklin's childhood bedroom thinking she's in the bathroom as she pisses into his old toy chest. An enviable Thanksgiving dinner!

In my novel *Sweet Adversity* I give myself the problem of having my Siamese twin Teddy lose his two front teeth by walking into a subway stanchion while drunk, and then having to thay everything after that with a lithp. Lisps, stutters, and stammers make for hard work in dialogue and almost never come off. But I had no choice, once Teddy walked into the steel stanchion. I chose to write in every ess sound as *th*, which caused me to listen hard to esses that don't hiss and so are not *th*. One reviewer boxed my ears for not being consistent with the lisp—but that was his own tin ear he belabored, since some esses sound as zee. You have to set up rules with lisps, stammers, and stutters, and listen precisely to your character's voice. In the scene below, the Siamese twins Leo-Teddy, a pair of horn-playing drunks of *modest* musical talent, have taken a job as social workers at Manhattan's Third World Metropolitan Hospital. Joined at the hip and now in their middle thirties, they have a common bloodstream. Leo joins Alcoholics Anonymous and goes eighty-nine days without a drink, but Teddy keeps boozing as usual. On their way to work this morning, Teddy loses the bridge for his front teeth while vomiting between moving subway cars, and splits his pants at the same time—a safety pin now holds his ass together as the twins write up new clients at the hospital. They've just interviewed a black woman with a cup-sized maggoty head wound and, in shock, turned her over to an intern. Reeling, Teddy thirsts for a quick hop to Tiger's nearby bar.

Leo-Teddy sighing at each other.

"Thith is my life! I felt those fuckin' worms right under my thkin!"

Leo looks out at a line of clients.

"Let the pithheads wait. Okay? *Right*, man. I need tequila. Let'th go."

A young Spanish girl with a baby waits in their doorway for her interview.

"Let's wait for Gerard."

"I can't thit here. I'm afraid there'll be worms wherever I lay my hand. I jutht wanna bang my head againtht the gong and thlowly thcream t'death! Ya know, *you* are jutht too weird for words. How can you thit here tho calmly, tho *coldly*, not feelin' anything? Huh? Let'th go." Teddy looks up at the girl. *"The habla ingles?"*

"Un poco, senor." She smiles graciously.

"No importante." Teddy rises in bliss toward Tiger's. "Have thith chair, mother, the man'll be right back."

She backs off from Teddy's eager eyes.

"Have a theat!" Teddy gives her *Dr. Strange.* "Here's a visual aid."

Stonebleak snow whips the playground, harsh wind molding kneebones. "Whoo, do I need tequila! Gotta get me thome new threads before I freeze my balls. I thpeak literally. Why not hit a Harlem pawnshop for thuits tonight?"

"You're gettin' your horn outta hock!"

Leo-Teddy draws stools together, Teddy crying, "Hit me with a triple, Tiger!" Beams at the bountiful tequila bottle on the pretty bar.

"All out," Tiger says, tossing the empty below the bar. "Somethin' else?"

"Ginger ale," Leo says.

Teddy droops, slack, lost, razored. "No more *tequila*?" Tragic eyes rove the whole pretty shelf, then Teddy stands, bitterly scanning the lower shelves of backup bottles. "UNH!" he grunts, lifeblood running down his stool. "Thith is a blow."

"What'll it be?" Tiger asks.

"Gee, don't you *thtock* tequila? That'th my favorite, Tiger."

Tiger waits under ring pics of himself as middleweight contender, handsome, redblond, nose, eyes, ears faintly swollen, forever. He shrugs. "We don't get that trade."

"*I* drink it. God, ya thtock Fockink gin and that'th a thpecialty item."

"I got that case at a discount." Tiger glances at three hatted men muttering in a dim corner. "Let's not argue," he rasps.

"Triple vodka and lemon. Uh, hundred proof."

Tiger sets up Teddy with a salt shaker and whole lemon in wedges, watching Teddy sniff at his shredded wet kleenex. "Murderouth potht-nasal drip," Teddy sighs. He pays for Leo, snorting at Leo's glass. "How d'ya drink that garbage day after day?"

Leo squints at the Fockink label. "Ain't easy."

"*Boy!*" Teddy laps salt from his fist, sucks wedge, belts half his vodka. "*Ahh!*—that really does hit the thpot." His eyes water. "But it'th not tequila." Eyes the Fockink label. "Remember Mama's collection of miniatures in the diningroom? Raspberry liqueur, banana, creme da cacao, creme de menthe—"

"—peach and apricot," Leo says.

"—yeah, an' Thouthern Comfort. Lemon Hart Jamaica rum—what a cabinet she had!—"

"—before we got into it—"

"—talk about thrawberry fields forever, it was like a thoda fountain with a fantathtic kick in every flavor."

Leo's nerves lift in a powerful wave of homefeelings for alcohol, a cell-deep blush for the past.

"I only wish—"

"What?"

"I wasn't givin' my first A.A. talk tomorrow night! Whattaya think I wish?"

"Idiot. Dya think *I'd* thqueal? It'th nithe t' have you as a compath for gettin' home thtraight—but I could give that up. Go ahead, have one."

"I don't want a drink, I want a drunk. I just wish—I'll stick to pot."

"Your choithe."

"The fuckin' pot don't reach me like it used to, though! I like that disorienting, synergistic high with the lush boosting the tea. That's a bitch t' give up! Let's get some LSD at Dr. Sunshine's tomorrow night."

"Tonight! Why wait?"

"No, tomorrow night I gotta have a clear head. Maybe I'll have one joint on the way to the meeting—just for the lift, so I can belt out my story. But—I think I could handle one beer right now. Maybe have another in three months, so I don't get a habit." Leo eyes the clock for months. "Maybe early Spring . . . Smell should be gone by the time I get home."

"Wanda can't tell *who* she's thmellin', you know that."

"Oh God, one beer. Just one bottle."

"Have a Canadian ale. More kick. Pep up the pot."

"Damn good idea." Leo's will cuts loose, a horse bolting downhill, he orders an ale, watches Tiger pour. Lifts the glass, focused utterly on the woody dark amber and brisk bubbles. Memoryless, guiltless, remorseless, sips off half the glass, sighs "AHHH!" right down to his soles, refills to the breaking brim.

Teddy, gaptooth grin. "How's that?"

"Instant hope," Leo whispers. "I feel *good*!" Lifting cells prick open, the soft punch of happiness, a brightening heavy soak of beautiful feelings. "Boy, one sip! 'S already goosing the tea. Floating! *Goot, goot!*—But one's enough."

"Ya know what A.A. thays. *No guilt* about drinkin'— it'th a wathte of energy. Drinking's the natural thtate of the alcoholic."

"Oh, it's a disease, it's not a matter of moral choice." Leo grins. "My God, that's good. If I were an alcoholic, I'd be in trouble."

"Don't feel guilty." Teddy gnaws his filtertip.

"I don't! Feel good. *Sprach Zarathustra!* Well—back to work!"

"I mean don't let thith little indithcretion interfere with your talk tomorrow night."

"Far from it! I feel a lot less tense already. Probably speak all the better—think of all those A.A.'s who can't drink even one beer and are committed to blind acceptance. But I'm an artist and I have to know both sides of the question. Right?"

Step into the street stript of its masks. "Eureka," Teddy whispers. Wonderbearing winter day, snow lathering heartbreak playground, high lifebush of tree limbs mirrored in Leo-Teddy's longing nerves, the high hospital haloed with humanity. Himalayan snows winding twilightyellow windows.

"This really is eternal life," Leo says.

"Welcome home."

—*Sweet Adversity* (1978),
Donald Newlove

Sweet Adversity embodies my final revisions for *Leo &*
Theodore (1972) and *The Drunks* (1974), as published in a
single-volume Avon paperback in 1978. I welcomed writing the scene above because it allowed me to draw on the
many slips I had getting sober and to dip into the beautiful
feelings that anchored my addiction. Leo, even though not
drinking, still smokes pot and can hardly be called sober,
despite his eighty-nine days off the bottle. Bound to Teddy
by a common bloodstream, Leo can't really get sober unless
Teddy hits bottom and joins him in recovery, though Leo
now, more or less, acts as his drunken brother's keeper.

This scene leaps from their office to the playground by
the hospital and then to stools in the bar. We're simply
there, as if by jump cuts: no hallway shot, no exit, no cross-
ing the streets, no entering the bar. Dialogue tells all, the
reader fills in the gaps. To keep their sense of wonder ever-
present, I boost all description to song level. With friendly
drunks like Leo-Teddy, a mix of Jekyll and Hyde and the
beloved Karloff monster, let the tongue sing out and everything glow in the synesthesia of alcohol, with the sensations of active addiction blooming with colors and sights
and sounds that cross over into feelings of immortality.
When I wrote this book, no other novel about Siamese
twins existed; I started from ground zero, guided only by
medical books and studies of freaks. The twins never think
of themselves as freaks, nor do I write about them as anything but human beings striving for goals as others strive. I
learned about them only bit by bit as I wrote, finding that
they have one touchy-feely skin, that their four eyes see in
wide screen, that they move in rhyme to avoid hurting
each other, that they glide rather than walk, and so on.
Writing about Leo-Teddy, a wonderful part of my life, can't

be stretched out with a third volume. Sensibilities move on. I've *done* Teddy the Boor with clients, his dismay that Tiger doesn't stock his favorite tequila, done Leo's seduction by his bad best friend, done his sobriety weakened by a brain lush with pot, I've dipped my senses back into the lift of the first drink ("the soft punch of happiness, a brightening heavy soak of beautiful feelings"), and all the rigamarole of alcoholic self-deception, done it, and am done with it. That's why we write, in part. To be done with it. Terry McMillan, I'm sure, delights in being done with that part of her life she mined for *Disappearing Acts*, and Shakespeare, I'm sure, delighted in being done with *Hamlet*. He never went back to that graveyard or to the sensibilities that told him Hamlet's letter should tell Ophelia that he was hers "as long as this machine is to him," that Hamlet sees himself not only as a machine but as some "quintessence of dust"—no other figure plucked from Shakespeare's spirit and endowed with sticky images of suicide and wrapped in black would bathe a skull with such rich wit:

HAMLET
[takes the skull]

Alas, poor Yorick! I knew him, Horatio—a fellow of infinite jest, of most excellent fancy. He hath borne me on his back a thousand times, and now how abhorred in my imagination it is! my gorge rises at it. Here hung those lips, that I have kissed I know not how oft. Where be your gibes now? your gambols? your songs? your flashes of merriment that were wont to set the table on a roar? Not one now to mock your own grinning? Quite chop-fallen [sunken-cheek'd]? Now get you to my lady's chamber, and tell her, let her paint an inch thick, to this favor she must come. Make her laugh at that. Prithee, Horatio, tell me one thing.

HORATIO

What's that, my lord?

HAMLET

Dost thou think Alexander looked o' this fashion i' the earth?

HORATIO

E'en so.

HAMLET

And smelt so? Pah!
[Throws down the skull]

—*Hamlet* V.i (1604),
William Shakespeare

Having thrown down the skull, Shakespeare's done with maggot wit and never returns to it on such a scale again. He'd done it, said what his grisly images and ironies demanded of him in his middle thirties, and turned to other things. True, he wrote *Macbeth* three years later, but *Macbeth*'s public music—and not witty at all, even with the squiffed doorkeeper. *Hamlet* strikes me as personal, written as much to unload Shakespearean darkness as to amuse the public. Its clowns dig graves, and in the court Osric and Rosencrantz and Guildenstern arise for Hamlet to sharpen his tongue on, pricking fashion and fickle friends, not to mention whetting his edge on Claudius, Gertrude, Polonius, and even Ophelia, whom he slaps with his poisonous view of women. Wild Bill is Hamlet, a soul gone black.

Many of Hamlet's great speeches about man ("What a piece of work is a man") and death, aside from "To be or not to be," fall into prose, as does Hamlet's wormwit about Polonius's body:

KING

Now, Hamlet, where's Polonius?

HAMLET

At supper.

KING

At supper! Where?

HAMLET

Not where he eats, but where he is eaten. A certain convocation of politic worms are e'en at him. Your worm is your only emperor for diet. We fat all creatures else to fat us, and we fat ourselves for maggots. Your fat king and your lean beggar is but variable service—two dishes, but to one table. That's the end.

KING

Alas, alas!

HAMLET

A man may fish with the worm that hath eat of a king, and eat of the fish that hath fed of that worm.

KING

What dost thou mean by this?

HAMLET

Nothing but to show you how a king may go a progress through the guts of a beggar.

KING

Where is Polonius?

HAMLET

In heaven. Send thither to see. If your messenger find him not there, seek him in the other place yourself. But

if, indeed, you find him not within this month, you shall
nose him as you go up the stairs into the lobby.

KING
[To Attendants]
Go seek him there.

HAMLET
He will stay till you come.

—IV.iii

When Wild Bill's deadly serious, as when dwelling on
flesh—sinful, too, too sullied, maggoty flesh—he likes
prose, as if saying, "Sniff this, life as it is—without music."
Well, as I say, after *Hamlet* he's done with it.

The English novelist Jane Austen (1775–1817) seemingly writes the same book over and over, and yet each is
unique. What we mistake for the same book lies in the narrow scope of her settings and sameness of social manners
from book to book. A clergyman's daughter, naturally
reserved, and very shy despite her great gift for fun both in
life and in her writing, she broke within a night her
engagement to a well-to-do suitor years younger than herself (she preferred another, whom she loved long after
hope was gone) and died at forty-two, a virgin. During
her lifetime she published four novels anonymously, and
two saw print later, as did lesser works. She revised greedily and wrote for the joy of it. She died unsung. Not un-
read, just obsessively unsung, with authorship her smiling
little secret.

Reason, taste, and virtue rule in Austen, though filtered
through a comic spirit. She writes as a realist in a world of
small country homes and villages yet to herald Byron,
Shelley, and Keats, whose rock band does not shake

England with its Romantic possibilities until Jane's last years. Her opinionated heroine in *Pride and Prejudice*, Elizabeth Bennet, mocks romantic verses to the prideful Darcy when told of a young lady who received them but lost her suitor.

> "And so ended his affection," said Elizabeth impatiently. "There has been many a one, I fancy, overcome in the same way. I wonder who first discovered the efficacy of poetry in driving away love!"
>
> "I have been used to considering poetry the *food* of love," said Darcy.
>
> "Of a fine, stout, healthy love it may. Everything nourishes what is strong already. But if it be only a slight, thin sort of inclination, I am convinced that one good sonnet will starve it entirely away."

"Everything nourishes what is strong already"—wonderful! Where did she get that line? And with what refreshing impatience Elizabeth hits that "starve it"—don't write *me* thin, sickly verses. A realist—in a day when women had no hope of escaping the family hearth but by marriage. As Elizabeth's father says on page two, Lizzy and her four unmarried sisters are "silly and ignorant like other girls; but Lizzy has more of a quickness than her sisters." Right at the top of her story, Austen strikes the note of women's restricted lives, their enforced ignorance, and later again characterizes them as silly. Having no dowries also traps the Bennet girls: the parsonage they live in so handsomely was entailed when Mr. Bennet inherited it and must be passed on to a male heir. Poor Mr. and Mrs. Bennet must answer to society and find husbands for these girls, who will otherwise drift into middle age as penniless spinsters. Ignorance and silliness confound the girls' endless gabble about the stock market of marriage, inheritances, men's uniforms, and correct manners. This may be comedy, but it's not farce, and the piercing wit of Austen's first sentence turns her theme upside down (she knows her story's about women chasing men): "It is a truth universally acknowledged, that a single man in possession of a good fortune, must be in want of a wife." She tells us this solemnly as if from a man's viewpoint—but woman's viewpoint wins, and the whole spirit of her story springs from that. No scene in this novel happens without a woman present.

While Austen suggests hard times hanging over the unmarried Bennets, she quickly sounds her theme of the proud Darcy and prejudiced Elizabeth (Elizabeth dislikes Darcy because of his pride) not coming together until they reverse their misreadings of each other. In their script for the two-hour MGM version of the novel, British novelist Aldous Huxley and Jane Murfin try to keep Austen's realism intact but find their work smothered by MGM's over-fussy costumes and the need to "open up" the Helen Jerome play from which the screenplay springs: director Robert Z. Leonard's camera demands action, movement, fast horses, great scenery, rich costumes, and interesting sets. The actors often rise above this humbug. The BBC-TV version from England, scripted by hard-edged feminist Fay Weldon and directed by Cyril Coke, runs about four hours and keeps closer to Austen, though its reverence and stillness dampen the story, despite the pertness of the actors. The great opening sentence, for example, delayed by five minutes and then put into Elizabeth's mouth, dies midair, through no fault of the actress.

The MGM version elides dances on two different days into one; I do something of the same in my fairly long excerpt from the novel so that we'll have the same information to set beside the two much briefer script excerpts. Young, well-to-do Mr. Bingley, the new renter of Netherfield Hall, brings with him to this dance his wealthy bachelor guest, Mr. Darcy. The dances, by the way, move quite slowly, with stateliness, no embraces, and gloved fingers merely touch.

Elizabeth Bennet had been obliged by the scarcity of the gentlemen to sit down for two dances; and during that part of the time, Mr. Darcy had been standing near enough for her to overhear a conversation between him and Mr. Bingley, who came from the dance for a few minutes to press his friend to join it.

"Come, Darcy," said he, "I must have you dance. I hate to see you standing about in this stupid manner. You had much better dance."

"I certainly shall not. You know how I detest it, unless I am particularly acquainted with my partner. At such an assembly as this, it would be insupportable. Your sisters are engaged, and there is not another woman in the room whom it would not be a punishment for me to stand up with."

"I would not be so fastidious as you are," cried Bingley, "for a kingdom! Upon my honor, I never met with so many pleasant girls in my life as I have this evening, and there are several of them you see uncommonly pretty."

"*You* are dancing with the only handsome girl in the room," said Mr. Darcy, looking at the eldest Miss Bennet [Elizabeth's sister Jane].

"Oh! she is the most beautiful creature I ever beheld! But there is one of her sisters sitting down just behind you, who is very pretty, and I dare say, very agreeable. Do let me ask my partner to introduce you."

"Which do you mean?" and turning round, he looked

for a moment at Elizabeth, till catching her eye, he withdrew his own and coldly said, "She is tolerable; but not handsome enough to tempt *me*; and I am in no humour at present to give consequence to young ladies who are slighted by other men. You had better return to your partner and enjoy her smiles, for you are wasting your time with me."

Mr. Bingley followed his advice. Mr. Darcy walked off; and Elizabeth remained with no very cordial feelings towards him. She told the story however with great spirit among her friends, for she had a lively, playful disposition, which delighted in anything ridiculous.

* * *

[THE SECOND DANCE DAYS LATER]

Mr. Darcy stood near [the dancers] in silent indignation at such a mode of passing the evening, to the exclusion of all conversation, and was too much engrossed by his own thoughts to perceive that Sir William Lucas was his neighbor, till Sir William thus began.

"What a charming amusement for young people this is, Mr. Darcy! There is nothing like dancing after all. I consider it as one of the first refinements of polished societies."

"Certainly, sir; and it has the advantage also of being in vogue amongst the less polished societies of the world. Every savage can dance."

* * *

"My dear Miss Eliza, why are you not dancing?—Mr. Darcy, you must allow me to present this young lady to you as a very desirable partner. You cannot refuse to dance, I am sure, when so much beauty is before you." And taking her hand, [Sir William] would have given it to Mr. Darcy, who, though extremely surprised, was not unwilling to receive it, when she instantly drew back, and said with some discomposure to Sir William,

"Indeed, sir, I have not the least intention of dancing. I entreat you not to suppose that I moved this way in order to beg for a partner."

Mr. Darcy with grave propriety requested to be allowed the honor of her hand; but in vain. Elizabeth was determined; nor did Sir William at all shake her purpose by his attempt at persuasion.

"You excel so much in the dance, Miss Eliza, that it is cruel to deny me the happiness of seeing you; and though this gentleman dislike the amusement in general, he can have no objection, I am sure, to oblige for one half hour."

"Mr. Darcy is all politeness," said Elizabeth, smiling.

"He is indeed—but considering the inducement, my dear Miss Eliza, we cannot wonder at his complaisance; for who would object to such a partner?"

Elizabeth looked archly, and turned away. Her resistance had not injured her with the gentleman, and he was thinking of her with some complacency, when thus accosted by Miss Bingley.

"I can guess the subject of your reverie."

"I should imagine not."

"You are considering how insupportable it would be to pass many evenings in this manner—in such society; and indeed I am quite of your opinion. I was never more annoyed! The insipidity and yet the noise; the nothingness and yet the self-importance of all these people! What would I give to hear your strictures on them!"

"Your conjecture is totally wrong, I assure you. My mind was more agreeably engaged. I have been meditating on the very great pleasure which a pair of fine eyes in the face of a pretty woman can bestow."

Miss Bingley immediately fixed her eyes on his face,

and desired he would tell her what lady had the credit of inspiring such reflections. Mr. Darcy replied with great intrepidity.

"Miss Elizabeth Bennet."

"Miss Elizabeth Bennet!" repeated Miss Bingley. "I am all astonishment. How long has she been such a favorite?—and pray when am I to wish you joy?"

"That is exactly the question which I expected you to ask. A lady's imagination is very rapid; it jumps from admiration to love, from love to matrimony in a moment. I knew you would be wishing me joy."

—*Pride and Prejudice* (1813),
Jane Austen

Let's go at once into the MGM version:

Elizabeth (Greer Garson) and her supposedly plain, newly married twenty-seven-year-old friend Mrs. Charlotte Collins (the lovely Karen Morley) sit alone in an alcove just off the dance floor as Darcy (Laurence Olivier) and Bingley (Bruce Lester) happen to loiter near them. The ladies overhear:

BINGLEY

Darcy, come! I hate to see you stalking about by yourself in this stupid manner. Why don't you dance?

DARCY

With whom? Your sister's engaged and there isn't another woman in the room that it wouldn't be a punishment for me to dance with.

BINGLEY

But the place is full of pretty girls!

DARCY

I've noticed only one and you seem to have monopolized her.

BINGLEY

Yes, isn't she lovely. But there's that sister of hers, Miss Elizabeth. They say she has quite a lively wit.

DARCY

Uh! A provincial young lady with a lively wit, heaven preserve us! And there's that mother of hers.

BINGLEY

It's not the mother you have to dance with, it's the daughter. She's charming.

DARCY

Yes, she looks tolerable enough. But I'm in no humor tonight to give consequence to the middle classes at play. *[They go off]*

ELIZABETH

What a charming man! Of all the arrogant, detestable snobs!

CHARLOTTE

Oh, but Lizzy, he *didn't* know you were listening.

ELIZABETH

What difference does it make? He would have said it just the same if he had. *[Imitating Darcy]* 'Oh, she looks tolerable enough, but I'm in no humor tonight to give consequence to the middle classes at play.' And to think how we badgered poor Pa-pa to get him here.

[Elizabeth sits aside by herself as Sir William Lucas talks about the dance with Darcy.]

DARCY

I was about to ask you, Sir William, if you would do me the kindness to introduce me to Miss Bennet?

SIR WILLIAM (E. E. Clive)

Oh, certainly. Dancing is a charming amusement for young people. In my opinion, it is one of the first refinements of a polished society.

DARCY

With the added advantage, sir, of being one of the first refinements of savages. Every Hottentot can dance.

SIR WILLIAM

Miss Elizabeth, may I have the honor to present Mr. Darcy? He is eager to invite you to dance.

DARCY

Now that you've been forewarned of my eagerness to dance with you, may I hope that you will do me the honor?

ELIZABETH

I am afraid that the honor of standing up with you, Mr. Darcy, is more than I can bear.

DARCY

Am I to understand that you *don't* wish to dance with me, Miss Bennet?

ELIZABETH

Sir, I am begging to be excused.

DARCY

The loss is mine, I'm sure.

ELIZABETH

You perhaps would know best about that, sir.

—*Pride and Prejudice* (1940),
script by Aldous Huxley and Jane Murfin,
from the play by Helen Jerome

And now the BBC-TV version. In this teleplay, Charlotte (Irene Richard), at last really quite plain, tells Elizabeth

(Elizabeth Garvie) that "happiness in marriage is entirely a matter of chance. It is best to know as little as possible of the defects of the person with whom you are to pass your life." Elizabeth now sits alone at the dance and overhears Bingley (Osmond Bullock) and Darcy (David Rantoul):

BINGLEY

Come, Darcy! I must have you dance. I hate to see you standing around in this stupid manner.

DARCY

To dance with such company as this assembly can afford would be insupportable. Saving your sisters, there's not a woman in the place it would not be a punishment to stand up with.

BINGLEY

The room is full of pleasant girls and some of them uncommonly pretty.

DARCY

There is the eldest Miss Bennet, perhaps, but you are dancing with her.

BINGLEY

Oh, she's the most beautiful creature I ever beheld. She has a sister!

DARCY

She has all too many sisters.

BINGLEY

Miss Elizabeth Bennet is charming.

DARCY

She is tolerable—but not handsome enough to tempt me. And I cannot after all give consequence to young ladies who are slighted by other men.

[AT THE SECOND DANCE DAYS LATER]

CHARLOTTE

Mr. Darcy admires you, Elizabeth.

ELIZABETH

Mr. Darcy!? He *does* overlisten to my conversations. Why?

CHARLOTTE

You better ask Mr. Darcy that yourself.

ELIZABETH

That would be impertinent. But if I am not impertinent soon, I shall grow afraid of him. He has a very satirical eye. Come along, Charlotte.

[Elizabeth and Charlotte go up to Mr. Darcy]

ELIZABETH

Do you not think, Mr. Darcy, I expressed myself remarkably well just now?

DARCY

You were talking of dancing and that always renders a woman eloquent.

ELIZABETH

You are severe on us.

[LATER]

SIR WILLIAM (Peter Howell)

There's nothing like dancing, sir! One of the first refinements of polished societies.

DARCY

It is certainly widespread. Every savage dances.

SIR WILLIAM

Here's Eliza! Why are you not dancing? Mr. Darcy, Miss Eliza! Mr. Darcy, you cannot refuse to dance when so much beauty is before you!

ELIZABETH

I have not the least intention of dancing. And I'm certainly not begging for a partner.

DARCY

Miss Bennet, I have the honor.

SIR WILLIAM

You excel so much in the dance, Miss Eliza, that Mr. Darcy, who in general dislikes the amusement, wishes to oblige.

ELIZABETH

[Moving away] Mr. Darcy is all politeness.

[Darcy moves to Miss Bingley]

MISS BINGLEY (Marsha Fitzalan)

I can guess!

DARCY

What?

MISS BINGLEY

You find it all so insupportable. So do I! Such insipidity and yet such noise, the nothingness and self-importance—

DARCY

No, I have been meditating upon the very great pleasure which a pair of fine eyes in the face of a pretty woman can bestow.

MISS BINGLEY

And who has inspired that?

DARCY

Miss Elizabeth Bennet.

MISS BINGLEY

I am awed in amazement! When am I to wish you joy?

DARCY

A lady's imagination is very rapid. It jumps from admiration to love, from love to matrimony in a moment.

—*Pride and Prejudice* (1988),
script by Fay Weldon

First, changes in the exclamations mean little—nor does the recasting of some lines, though I especially like Huxley/Murfin's "stalking about" for Austen's "I hate to see you standing about in this stupid manner." MGM's "Hottentot" on top of "savage" hardly matters, but Weldon's sharpness with this speech loses wit altogether. Among the larger changes, Huxley/Murfin decide to add Charlotte right off, while Austen and Weldon have Elizabeth overhear Darcy alone at the first dance and delay Charlotte's entrance until the second dance days later. The MGM version trims all the speeches and shortens the two dances to one, while Weldon, having four hours to fill and be faithful, refines and adds lines from elsewhere. I could have run all three sets of speeches in parallel—but here I'll let your own interest guide you in how deeply you wish to look into them. We miss the actors from these scripts. Olivier reads Darcy more warmly than Rantoul, and at his first entrance plants Darcy's later fall from pride. Elizabeth Garvie's Elizabeth for the BBC has Austenish reserve, while Greer Garson adds a snippy charm that with sumptuous MGM lighting leaves her ravishing and much too beautiful for the role—in this case a flaw on the side of the angels, since she steals every frame she's in—and I find the idea that she plays the spirit of a woman who will die a virgin at forty-two, well, *insupportable*. The scripts make small gains in pace and more natural speech, and the actors add flesh and subtlety, but Austen's dialogue, however stiff, sends down roots even the BBC-TV lacks time to grow. Novel dialogue simply moves at a slower pace in a different world than dramatic dialogue, even when the lines mirror each other. The ear catches them faster than the eye, but the eye looks into them more richly. And, whatever merits the actors bring, "trash"—ha!—like *The Maltese Falcon*, with its strong storyline, leaps more easily and freshly to film than do *Anna Karenina* and *Swann in Love*.

E. M. Forster himself, without much dialogue, reports my favorite scene in the film of his novel *Howards End*—the face-off between Miss Margaret Schlegel and her fiancé, the widower Mr. Henry Wilcox, over his affair ten years earlier with a twenty-three-year-old slut in Cyprus. Ruth Prawer Jhabvala, the scriptwriter, does a strong, intelligent job of lifting dialogue from Forster's thoughts for a lengthy coming together of Margaret and Henry. This dreary patching up of their feelings apparently goes on for hours—it takes three fade-outs in five minutes to suggest the passage of time in this scene! Oddly enough, Forster's clear statement here, that Henry fakes his shame, doesn't come through in the film. The actors play about with Henry's furtiveness but don't hammer home in words that Henry's making up new defenses as he admits to old sins and that Margaret *may* be cheating on her emancipated womanhood, thoughts I didn't catch until rereading the book. What draws us so strongly into humiliation scenes? Caught up in Henry's soul-baring, we miss its undercurrent of sham and his Victorian posturing.

In an earlier scene, the widower Wilcox invites Margaret to see his huge town house, a vast pile of rooms. Their own house being lost, would she and her brother and sister like to rent this one? But Henry's shamming here as well: after looking through all the richly furnished rooms, they stop in the drawing room and he asks her to marry him.

But the proposal was not to rank among the world's great love scenes.

"Miss Schlegel"—his voice was firm—"I have had you up on false pretenses. I want to speak about a much more serious matter than a house."

Margaret almost answered: "I know—"

"Could you be induced to share my—is it probable—"

"Oh, Mr. Wilcox!" she interrupted, holding the piano and averting her eyes. "I see, I see. I will write to you afterwards if I may."

He began to stammer. "Miss Schlegel—Margaret— you don't understand."

"Oh yes! Indeed, yes!" said Margaret.

"I am asking you to be my wife."

So deep already was her sympathy that when he said, "I am asking you to be my wife," she made herself give a little start. She must show surprise if he expected it. An immense joy came over her. It was indescribable. It had nothing to do with humanity, and most resembled the all-pervading happiness of fine weather. Fine weather is due to the sun, but Margaret could think of no central radiance here. She stood in his drawing-room happy, and longing to give happiness. On leaving him she realized that the central radiance had been love.

"You aren't offended, Miss Schlegel?"

"How could I be offended?"

There was a moment's pause. He was anxious to get rid of her, and she knew it. She had too much intuition to look at him as he struggled for possessions that money cannot buy. He desired comradeship and affection, but he feared them, and she, who had taught herself only to desire, and could have clothed the struggle with beauty, held back, and hesitated with him.

"Goodbye," she continued. "You will have a letter from me—I am going back to Swanage tomorrow."

"Thank you."

"Goodbye, and it's you I thank."

"I may order the motor round, mayn't I?"

"That would be most kind."

"I wish I had written instead. Ought I to have written?"

"Not at all."

"There's just one question—"

She shook her head. He looked a little bewildered, and they parted.

They parted without shaking hands: she had kept the interview, for his sake, in tints of the quietest grey. Yet she thrilled with happiness ere she reached her own house. . . . As she sat trying to do accounts in her empty house, amidst beautiful pictures and noble books, waves of emotion broke, as if a tide of passion was flowing through the night air . . .

—*Howards End* (1910),
E. M. Forster

But no "I love yous" in the dialogue. Forster himself reserves the right to tell of the feelings between his characters. He allows neither to speak freely. So the big patching-it-up humiliation scene comes out so heavily Forster, so little Margaret and Henry speaking for themselves. Forster himself wants to have their feelings! A reserved, shy man, he sets his characters in motion, gives them chat and passions, but keeps to himself the rich dirt of their feelings, digging his fingers into their psyches without their help and sucking everything up for himself. Nice work if you can get it.

Margaret does the accounts as Forster writes of her bursting heart. In her empty house, where Forster lusts to place her, she strives for some ledgerlike understanding of her debts and credit as "amidst beautiful pictures and noble books, waves of emotion broke, as if a tide of passion was flowing through the night air." Boy, that's not romance writing, where Melissa sips her rosé, throws open the veranda windows, and steps out under the stars, still gripped by Jacques's passion in the vine-leaved gazebo. What's the difference between Forster's feelings and that romance writer's? Aren't feelings feelings, however you prick them to life? Well, the romance writer just drifts and plays with himself, but Forster joins his male and female selves at the deeps of his being, sets Margaret to reasoning like Henry over the accounts, then brings in the night air to suggest the tenderness of Henry's intuitive female side calling her male reasoning down into the darks of the rupturing unconscious. Is this love out of darkness and marriage on the night air a cliché on my part, out of Jung and D. H. Lawrence—or does Forster really make himself fertile, self-pollinating, a writer heavy with child, gravely alive with a birth taking place in every joint of his fingers and brightness of nerve balled within him? Cliché or not, I know I feel mazy as a woman when feeling for my next thought, even in this book, as well as focused as a man in seeking words that chop wood and end thoughts with a hard beat. Whatever, with self-sex like that, Forster doesn't need to slather Margaret with rapturous fantasy.

So let's see how Ruth Prawer Jhabvala handles this scene for director James Ivory. They play it on a huge staircase between floors, with the powerful Mr. Wilcox

(Anthony Hopkins) looming five or six steps above Margaret (Emma Thompson). An Oscar-winner for this role, Thompson plays Margaret—a virgin in her middle thirties—rather younger, though still strongly sensible and able to feel her way into Wilcox without loss of self.

HENRY

Have you ever been lonely, Miss Schlegel?

MARGARET

I soon shall. Horribly. It's heartbreaking to leave one's old home. Look how high this ceiling must be.

HENRY

Yes. It must be over thirty feet. No, forty, I should think. Perhaps even more. Uh, Miss Schlegel, uh, I've had you up here on false pretenses. I want to speak to you on a more serious matter than the house. Um, do you think you could be induced to, uh, share—I mean, is it at all probable that—

MARGARET

Oh yes, I see.

HENRY

Miss Schlegel. Margaret. I don't think you quite understand.

MARGARET

Oh, yes. Indeed, yes.

HENRY

I'm asking you to be my wife.

MARGARET

Yes. I know, I know.

HENRY

Are you offended?

MARGARET

How could I be offended?

HENRY

Perhaps I should have written first?

MARGARET

No, no. Rather, you will receive a letter from me.

HENRY

Thank you.

MARGARET

Not at all. It's you I thank.

HENRY

Uh, should I order the motor around now?

MARGARET

That would be most kind. *[Walks back up stairs, kisses him. Walks down. Takes up hat and gloves, with a look back. Exit.]*

—*Howards End* (1992),
script by Ruth Prawer Jhabvala

Jhabvala/Ivory follow Forster's motto for *Howards End*, "Only connect . . . ," and connect up everything in the script. For me their main shortcoming lies in not showing the full craftiness Forster gives Mr. Wilcox. Earlier in the novel, the late Mrs. Wilcox befriended Margaret, they grew quite close, and Mrs. Wilcox willed Howards End, her rebuilt farmhouse, to Margaret. But Mr. Wilcox burned that scribbled codicil and kept Howards End for himself and his son Charles, denying it to the unwitting Margaret. In the confessional scene later, Mr. Wilcox makes no mention that he carried on his affair with the slut in Cyprus behind

Mrs. Wilcox's back. He not only betrayed Margaret's late friend, he then defends his acts by calling himself "a bad lot" and sighing that Margaret's "found him out" and so on, all shams that have slyly allowed him to cheat on his wife without remorse—and now bear the unsaid thought that he'll go right on popping tarts when married to Margaret. We must remember that Forster wrote *Howards End* in 1909–10 and that, despite widespread death in childhood, the double standard kept down the number of children in families, though Victorian families often had six or more children, with wives withholding their favors during the later months of each pregnancy. Famous prudes these Victorians, calling chair legs "limbs," but those lamplight folks spent more hours in bed than couples today busy with their cars, movies, and electronics. Wealthy Mr. Wilcox buys any standard that pleases him. What's more, in the proposal scene on the stairs, he quite forgets already having cheated Margaret out of Howards End, about which he says nothing while asking for her hand nor while patching things up about his slut. Yes, the novel sees the well-spoken Mr. Wilcox really as a bad lot—Margaret at last finds him "rotten at the core"—and he offers no turn of character until very ill in the last chapter.

Jhabvala trims out very little from Forster's version of the proposal but adds the kiss, which may violate the underlying business-merger affect of the scene—Margaret has few illusions about Mr. Wilcox's getting and spending. And yet the kiss replaces Forster's beautiful pilfering from Tolstoy.* "An immense joy came over her. It was indescrib-

---

*At eighty-two in 1910, Tolstoy loomed as the most admired writer on earth, not only for his grip on women (the raptures of Natasha Rostova and Anna Karenina), but also for his larger soul-shiftings about the power of love. If you steal, steal big.

able. It had nothing to do with humanity, and most resembled the all-pervading happiness of fine weather. Fine weather is due to the sun, but Margaret could think of no central radiance here. She stood in his drawing-room happy, and longing to give happiness. On leaving him she realized that the central radiance had been love."

Do we miss the novel's big arias on death, cause and effect, and horror? Might a narrator have supplied these, if only in brief? Can a movie this busy handle these larger thoughts? Well, brilliantly, for me at least, the wonderful music track, its gigantic crashing chords underscoring the cracks in society and splitting seams of the universe, replaces much of Forster's overarching dismay. *Howards End* saw print when Forster was only thirty-one. Nearly fifty years later he thought about the novel again and wrote this note to himself:

> *Howards End* my best novel and approaching a good novel. Very elaborate and all pervading plot that is seldom tiresome or forced, range of characters, social sense, wit, wisdom, colour. Have only just discovered why I don't care for it: not a single character in it for whom I care. . . . Perhaps the house in *HE*, for which I did once care, took the place of people and now that I no longer care for it, their barrenness has become evident. I feel pride in the achievement, but cannot love it, and occasionally the swish of the skirts and the non-sexual embraces irritate. . . .
>
> —*Commonplace Book*, May 1958

On the strength of his latest work, *All the Pretty Horses*, the first novel in his "Border Trilogy," novelist Cormac McCarthy is among the greatest descriptive writers alive, and his dialogue is hardly less to be envied. Born in Tennessee, he writes about the South and the West, but I don't think of him as a regional writer. My favorite piece by him has long been a ninety-minute television script, "The Gardener's Son," broadcast on public television in the middle or late seventies, which I've seen twice and would dearly love to see again. Since it's not possible to talk about McCarthy's dialogue without speaking of the thunder of the land that rises up into his characters, here is a glowing sample both of his descriptive strength and his dialogue. In 1946, three teenage cowpokes, John Grady Cole, Lacey Rawlins, and—much the youngest—Jimmy Blevins, ride by horse from Texas into Mexico:

By early evening all the sky to the north had darkened and the spare terrain they trod had turned a neuter gray as far as eye could see. They grouped in the road at the top of a rise and looked back. The storm front towered about them and the wind was cool on their sweating faces. They slumped bleary-eyed in their saddles and looked at one another. Shrouded in the black thunderheads the distant lightning glowed mutely like welding seen through foundry smoke. As if repairs were under way at some flawed place in the iron dark of the world.

It's fixin to come a goodn, said Rawlins

I caint be out in this, said Blevins

Rawlins laughed and shook his head. Listen at this, he said.

Where do you think you're goin to go? said John Grady.

I don't know. But I got to get somewheres.

Why cant you be out in it?

On account of the lightnin.

Lightnin?

Yeah.

Damn if you don't look about halfway sober all of a sudden, said Rawlins.

You afraid of lightnin? said John Grady.

I'll be struck sure as the world.

Rawlins nodded at the canteen hung by its strap from the pommel of John Grady's saddle. Don't give him no more of that shit. He's comin down with the DT's.

It runs in the family, said Blevins. My grandaddy was killed in a minebucket in West Virginia it run down in the hole a hunnerd and eighty feet to get him it couldn't even wait for him to get to the top. They had to wet down the bucket to cool it fore they could get him out of it, him and two other men. It fried em like bacon. My daddy's older brother was blowed out of a derrick in the Batson Field in the year nineteen and four, cable rig with a wood derrick but the lightnin got him anyways and him not nineteen year old. Great uncle on my mother's side—mother's side, I said—got killed on a horse and it never singed a hair on that horse and it killed him graveyard dead they had to cut his belt off him where it welded the buckle shut and I got a cousin aint but four years oldern me was struck down in his own yard comin from the barn and it paralyzed him all down one side and melted the fillins in his teeth and soldered his jaw shut.

I told you, said Rawlins. He's gone completely dipshit.

They didnt know what was wrong with him. He'd just twitch and mumble and point at his mouth like.

That's a out and out lie or I never heard one, said Rawlins.

Blevins didnt hear. Beads of sweat stood on his forehead. Another cousin on my daddy's side it got him it set his hair on fire. The change in his pocket burned through and fell out on the ground and set the grass alight. I done been struck twice how come me to be deaf in this one ear. I'm double bred for death by fire. You got to get away from anything metal at all. You don't know what'll get you. Brads in your overalls. Nails in your boots.

Well, what do you intend to do?

He looked wildly toward the north. Try and outride it, he said. Only chance I got.

Rawlins looked at John Grady. He leaned and spat. Well, he said. If there was any doubt before I guess that ought to clear it up.

You cant outride a thunderstorm, said John Grady. What the hell is wrong with you?

It's the only chance I got.

> —*All the Pretty Horses* (1992),
> Cormac McCarthy

Perfection! Deep-dish description, memorable comedy, each character anchored into his voice, and all of it fresh as spring scallions. McCarthy glides slyly from his big image of black thunderheads and distant lightning glowing "mutely like welding seen through foundry smoke. As if repairs were under way at some flawed place in the iron dark of the world"—into the tall tales about lightning Jimmy Blevins swears are his family legend. Sweat-beaded Jimmy next strips naked and tries to outride the lightning. Unlike Mark Twain, who might give us tall stories like Jimmy Blevins's, McCarthy keeps a straight face rehearsing the boy's fears, framing them with the blackened heavens and telling them to us just as Jimmy sees them, though Rawlins thinks Jimmy's drunk or dipshit—"Well, he said. If there was any doubt before I guess that ought to clear it up."

John Grady, the novel's hero, is straight man to Blevins as the boy's imagination explodes and races with Acts of

God, while Rawlins comments with droll asides. Not only here but elsewhere, Rawlins's wonderful comic turns hang from his leaping ahead of the obvious and looking backward from a plateau of plain common sense and hard-bitten cowboy wisdom—made even funnier by his being only seventeen.

Why does McCarthy do away with quote marks on dialogue and apostrophes in certain contractions? Or sometimes leap from past tense to mock present by stuffing a paragraph full of lively gerunds ("The laminar bands of color to the west bleeding out under hammered clouds. A sudden violetcolored hooding of the earth")?* For a fresh-looking, fresh-sounding page, rather squirmy and original, especially in description that flows with fantasy or poetry and sometimes runs ten or twelve lines without a comma. He sinks us into the page by demanding attention to each word. Don't skim, you'll drown, without a quote mark to save you. Does he conserve language and also charge his line by pruning away jabber and "he saids" and "she saids"? Hell, yes. But dialogue without quote marks demands extra care from the writer as well, so that at times, mid-paragraph, the reader hears at once a switch from dialogue to description. This device takes practice (many midnight hours!) and, often, endless revision so that the bare-looking page never strains the reader and flows smoothly to the palm, so to speak. Meanwhile, apostrophes fade from n't (not), lost g's, and from other words, but not from possessives or shortened verbs, which avoids misreadings of Ill for I'll and grotesqueries such as hes for he's. Much of this was introduced into English fiction early this century by George

---

*Laminar, as in laminated, means plated or scaled; I see clouds hammered into leaves or layers as if by a goldsmith and plated with blood, though the echo of laminar in hammered rings pictures into the ear as well as the eye.

Bernard Shaw and by James Joyce's *A Portrait of the Artist as a Young Man*, as were dropped commas in *Ulysses*, then picked up thirty years later by Ross Lockridge, Jr., for *Raintree County*, and two decades after that by myself in *The Painter Gabriel*. Like the triple somersault, new ways should always look easy, natural, and strike the reader as improvements. Shoulda been done like this all the time. These damned stylists, you see, are determined that you hear their words, not just stare at them. Any hack can whittle grammar into skimmable paragraphs. Only stylists give these clacking wooden analogs to human thought called sentences the pulse of music.

Let's end on a heavenly piece of dialogue by Ernest Hemingway. During his lifetime, many thought Hemingway's dialogue the world's best. It looked perfect for film. Too often, though, when filmed, it came out stilted, arch, and phony. Even the wisecracking dialogue of the two killers in his short story "The Killers"—a work of immense originality when first printed in 1927, then copied without end by scriptwriters for Warner Brothers crime movies in the thirties—rings hollow when acted. Worse, since he pissed on Hollywood and would not write screenplays, his dialogue knitted poorly with that by scriptwriters less alive to his characters than he. For that matter, a short story *is* a short story and the soul-shift of "The Killers"—Nick Adams's disillusionment with life when faced by two armed thugs set on murdering a man—gets lost when filmed with the thugs and melodrama forefront. The dialogue of his unactable dud play *The Fifth Column* commits its actors to laughable posturing, while that in *For Whom the Bell Tolls* is often solid wax.

Not many novelists become good playwrights, though Tolstoy did, and fewer novelists write good screenplays, and fewer still good screenplays from their own novels. An ear for staged dialogue, like an ear for poetry, doesn't grow overnight—and often doesn't grow. Refitting Ring Lardner's clipped sports talk and wisecracks to his own needs demanded that Hemingway—to be original—find fresh settings outside the ballpark and (aside from his earliest autobiographical short stories) fresh speakers not from small-town America or even New York but rather Americans and Europeans adrift in France and Spain and Italy. His humorless heroes, having beaten death, stand in bright daylight, supersensible to nature after being in some way maimed, and now sleep edgily, blistered by memories of horror and violence. Death always brightens Hemingway's eye. But his dialogue rings untrue when parted from his ice-clear sketchwork and reframed for film.

This passage comes from the end of *A Farewell to Arms*. The American hero, Frederic Henry, deserts his ambulance unit on the Italian front during World War I and takes his lover, a pregnant British nurse, to Switzerland. In this scene they have just reunited at Stresa before rowing to freedom across Lake Como. In the billiard room of a hotel, Frederic meets his old friend Count Greffi. Once a diplomat, the beautifully mannered Count, ninety-four, his hair and mustache white, still gives birthday parties, the great social event of Milan. "He was living to be one hundred years old and played a smoothly fluent game of billiards that contrasted with his own ninety-four-year-old brittleness." They play and, despite a handsome handicap for Frederic, the Count beats him. The Count keeps two bottles of champagne icing as they play and at last has a chilled fifth uncorked.

Count Greffi smiled and turned the glass with his fingers. "I had expected to become more devout as I grow older but somehow I haven't," he said. "It is a great pity."

"Would you like to live after death?" I asked and instantly felt a fool to mention death. But he did not mind the word.

"It would depend on the life. This life is very pleasant. I would like to live forever," he smiled. "I very nearly have."

We were sitting in the deep leather chairs, the champagne in the ice-bucket and our glasses on the table between us.

"If you ever live to be as old as I am you will find many things strange."

"You never seem old."

"It is the body that is old. Sometimes I am afraid I will break off a finger as one breaks a stick of chalk. And the spirit is no older and not much wiser."

"You are wise."

"No, that is the great fallacy; the wisdom of old men. They do not grow wise. They grow careful."

"Perhaps that is wisdom."

"It is a very unattractive wisdom. What do you value most?"

"Some one I love."

"With me it is the same. That is not wisdom. Do you value life?"

"Yes."

"So do I. Because it is all I have. And to give birthday parties," he laughed. "You are probably wiser than I am. You do not give birthday parties."

We both drank the wine.

[As they part, Frederic says:]

"Thank you. And I hope you will live forever."

"Thank you. I have. And if you ever become devout,

pray for me if I am dead. I am asking several of my friends to do that. I had expected to become devout myself but it has not come." I thought he smiled sadly but I could not tell. He was so old and his face was very wrinkled, so that a smile used so many lines that all gradations were lost.

—*A Farewell to Arms* (1929),
Ernest Hemingway

Could that be improved? Not by me. Why is it so wonderful? First, it's about life and death, and the seeming failure of age to bring wisdom to an old man who has looked forward to becoming devout and yet failed to do so. And not just an old man but an almost mythically old man whose billiard game still flows from ball to ball though he dreams of his fingers breaking like chalk. The figure of Count Greffi, and his straightforwardness, ravish us. His great age waters our spirits. And Count Greffi doesn't just mention his faded hope that he might come closer to God with great age, he repeats it, asking Frederic to pray for him even as he has asked others to do so. But—his gaiety, iced champagne, and endless birthday parties charm us, suggesting that gaiety itself is wisdom. Also, the thought they talk about, God and the afterlife, leaves us aware that neither man much believes in either subject, so that when Catherine, Frederic's beloved, dies of blood poisoning following labor, her death hits us with greater force. She is the goat offered up on the altar of Hemingway's tragic sense.

The dialogue runs down the page like brook water. Nothing veils us from the Count and Frederic. We don't rush, we want to hear every syllable, await eagerly each fresh line. We soak up the shadows that make each word bold. Hemingway clearly feels the breath of the gods giving him this amazing little passage at story's end, and that lifts his novel to high bloom. In 1917 at Stresa he chanced into Count Giuseppi Greppi (1819–1921), the real Count Greffi, who is actually ninety-eight, not ninety-four, when Frederic meets him at Stresa, and twelve years later Hemingway uses the meeting much as you or I might describe a champagne night spent with old Cary Grant at Aspen. Does Frederic ask the deeper questions he might? He does his best but stays within character and pretends to little wisdom beyond love of his child-heavy nurse and in this scene acts simply as straight man to Count Greffi, or Hamlet to the wise gravedigger. And we admire the Count, his humor ("I would like to live forever. I very nearly have"), his ease with Frederic, and his keen eye for what is wisdom and what isn't. Hemingway, now thirty, grafts a Frederic in his middle twenties onto the perils and feelings Hemingway knew at twenty while serving as a uniformed canteen worker with the Red Cross on the Italian front. How wise may he allow Frederic to be—as wise as himself at thirty? Unlike Private Henry Fleming in a novel much admired by Hemingway, Stephen Crane's *The Red Badge of Courage* (1895), a recruit who can't see past the patch of ground he's fighting on (but who also deserts like Frederic Henry, if only for a while), Frederic has a very long view of war, a weariness mixed with postwar cynicism, and asks and answers some very big questions midnovel about the meaning of war and about making his own separate peace with both sides in the war. The level of wisdom heroes draw from earlier parts of one's life remains a balancing act for all writers. Hemingway himself, a famous thirty-year-old writer, might have engaged Count Greffi more deeply—but would that be Frederic? As it is, we wonder how much of this dialogue Hemingway savored and saved from real life and how much came to him as he wrote. I feel we never need real people for dialogue, only their tone of voice as a compass leading us line by line toward human shapes emerging from speech.

Lastly, Hemingway gets one breath beating between his ribs and the reader's. Come with me, he says, I have something to tell you about a very old man who is so old and whose face is so wrinkled that a smile gets lost in the gradations of his wrinkles. He casts the writer's spell. We listen to grand storytelling that lives entirely in invented voices.

And here we are. I too had hoped to become very devout, know spiritual secrets, and with my writing crack open some starry door whose draft carries scent from a farther world. But it has not come. What has come, though, is pleasure, endless, replenishing, uplifting pleasure from writing, the one spiritual life granted me, aside from friendships and marriage. My pleasure wells from below the waking mind and feeds me with the joy of the word that catches the windowlight, puts highlights on eyeballs, and gives life. This pleasure tells me the feelings flowing to and fro between us, my feelings, your feelings, come from some higher force using me for its larger purpose of helping us both feel more deeply, with barer nerves and richer minds and stronger hearts, a purpose I grasp dimly and hear only in the hints of my words as they herd and leap like deer down the page.

My heart hides and yet bounds around inside and says let's be playful and it tells me to leap and invent the best possible farewell for it to speak in these pages. So here is a whole Thanksgiving table of voices I've become one with in writing this book. I hear Count Greffi's charming failure to become devout as he chats with Frederic Henry, I hear Forster's worser self, Mr. Wilcox, ask to marry the reasonable Margaret, who also abides in Forster. Here in a cab sit Rod and Marlon, or Charley and Terry Malloy, with Terry crying, "You don't understand! I coulda had class! I coulda been a contender! I coulda *been* somebody. Instead of a bum, which is what I am, let's face it." I hear Jake La Motta ask his brother Joey, "Did you ever fuck my wife?" "What!?" "You fucked my wife?" "How could you ask me a question like that? How could you ask me, I'm your brother. You asked me that? Where do you get your balls big enough to ask *me* that?" I hear Yossarian ask Doc Daneeka, "Can't you ground someone who's crazy?" "Oh, sure. I have to. There's a rule saying I have to ground any- one who's crazy." I hear Sam Spade tell Casper Gutman, "Let's talk about the black bird." "All right, sir, let's. Let's. This is going to be the most astounding thing you've ever heard of, sir, and I say this, knowing that a man of your cal- ibre and your profession must have known some astound- ing things in his time." I hear a trembling Louis Calhern as the crooked lawyer Emmerich tell his private detective, "Bob—I'm broke! That's the plain, simple fact. Finished. Bankrupt. . . . It's true. . . . Every time I turn around it costs thousands of dollars, ten thousand here, ten thousand there." I hear Roseanne Conner sigh as her sister Jackie leaves for the police academy, "Well, she's a big girl now." I hear Pozzo shouting at Didi and Gogo: "Have you not done tormenting me with your accursed time! It's abominable! When! When! One day, is that not enough for you? . . . They give birth astride of a grave, the light gleams an instant, then it's night once more." I hear George Sanders as Addison de Witt: "Margo, as you know, I've lived in the theater as a Trappist monk lives in his faith. I have no other world, no other life." I hear Noel Coward's Elyot tell his ex- wife Amanda, in the cruelly deceptive moonlight, "You're looking very lovely you know, in this damned moonlight. Your skin is clear and cool, and your eyes are shining, and you're growing lovelier and lovelier every second as I look at you. You don't hold any mystery for me, darling, do you mind? There isn't a particle of you that I don't know, remember, and want." I hear the French mime Baptiste's wife tell his lover Garance, "How easy it must be! . . . Easy to go away . . . and then to come back, missed. Time works for you and you come back, all fresh, and made more beautiful by memory." I hear Meryl Streep's Susan Traherne tell Sting's Mick Halloran, "Well, I'm looking for a father. I want to have a child. Look, it really is much easier than it sounds. Marriage is not involved, or even looking after it. You don't even have to see the pregnancy through. Conception would be the end of the job." I hear Jack Nicholson's Francis Phelan shout in a midnight alley at Meryl Streep's Helen Archer, "I'LL SHOW YOU WHAT I'M GONNA DO! I'm gonna knock you across that goddamn street!" "YEAH-H! You're stuPENDous—and colossal!" I hear Robert Taylor's Armand Duval give Greta Garbo's Marguerite Gautier a copy of *Manon Lescaut* with the warning "But it's rather sad. She dies in the end." "Well, then, I'll keep it but I won't read it. I don't like sad thoughts. However, we all die. So perhaps this will be sold someday at an auction after my death." I hear Marilyn's Cherie tell Eileen Heckart's Vera where she's going according to her map, "*HOLLYWOOD AND VI-INE!* Look, straight as an arrow, *phsheww-w!*—Hollywood and Vine!" I hear Marilyn's tipsy Elsie Marina tell Olivier's Regent of Carpathia, "I don't know why I was so nervous tonight . . . I thought I was going to have a real struggle with myself . . . if anyone knows about this love stuff, this guy will. Ha ha ha! . . . Oh, well." I hear Takashi Shimura's Mr.

Watanabe, with gastric cancer, tell the writer of trashy novels he's drinking with that alcohol's a poor form of suicide and the writer reply, "I'm only a hack writer. . . . But you're a fine man, you're fighting against death—that's what impresses me. . . . Man must have a greed for life." I hear Michael Gambon's Philip Marlow, wholly aflame with psoriasis and wracked with arthritis, now at the end of his tether, abandon all cynicism in a crying and laughing orgy of truth-telling, "I'd like—Christ, I'd—like to get out of it. I don't want—I can't—listen—I can *not* stand this any more . . . ooh it hurts my jaw and God! Talk about the Book of—the Book of Job I'm a prisoner inside my oooh own skin and and and bones—" I hear Charles Boyer's Don Juan tell Charles Laughton's Devil, "Were I not possessed with a purpose beyond my own I had better be a plowman than a philosopher; for the plowman . . . rejoices in the wife of his bosom with less misgiving. This is because the philosopher is in the grip of the Life Force." I hear Jimmy Stewart's Kralik the store manager tell Margaret Sullavan's Klara the clerk that he's her sweetheart pen pal, and she stares at him as at a ghost as he says, tremblingly, "Dear Friend!" "You—Dear Friend?" "Are you disappointed?" "Psychologically I'm very confused—but personally I don't feel bad at all!" I hear Betty Hutton's tearful Trudy Kockenlocker tell Eddie Bracken's Norville, who under stress sees spots, about her seducer, "His name had a Z in it—I *think*—I don't know. I've thought so much about it. The more I think about it the less I can remember." "Well, that's the terriblest thing I ever—what's your father gonna say when he finds out and ya can't—I mean, and ya haven't any husband—any proof! I mean, any—WHO'S HE GONNA—THE SPOTS!" I hear Jeff Daniels's dual role as Tom Baxter the screen image argues with Gil Shepherd the actor who created him and who begs Mia Farrow's Cecilia to tell Tom to go back up into the screen, "Will you tell him to go back? Tell him you, tell him that you don't love him. Tell him you *can't* love him. He's fictional! You want to waste your time with a fictional character?" I hear Bengt Ekerot's black-clad Death ask Max von Sydow's Hamletic knight, "You want guarantees?" "Call it whatever you like. Is it so cruelly inconceivable to grasp God with the senses? Why should he hide himself in a mist of half-spoken promises and unseen miracles?" I hear Nina tell the writer Trigorin, "But . . . inspiration!—the process of creation!—these *must* give you sublime and happy moments." "Before they pass they do. And looking over proofs is pleasant. But as soon as a thing is published my heart sinks. The damned thing's a failure! a botch—I should never have written it." I hear the stripped and hopeless facts of Herman Broder's mess as he phones his resurrected first wife from a 2:00 A.M. Broadway cafeteria in a blizzard and Tamara asks, "Where are your wives?" "They're both not speaking to me." I hear Dominique Francon posturing to Howard Roark, "I have hurt you today. I'll do it again. I'll come to you whenever I have beaten you—whenever I know that I have hurt you—and I'll let you own me. . . . What do you say now?" "Take your clothes off." I hear Leo Genn as Starbuck cry to Peck's Ahab, "To be enraged with a dumb brute that struck thee out of instinct is blasphemous." "Speak not to me of blasphemy, man. I'd strike the sun if it insulted me. Look you, Starbuck. All visible things are but as pasteboard masks. Some inscrutable yet reasoning thing puts forth the moulding of their features. The white whale tasks me. He *heaps* me. Yet he is but a mask. It is the thing behind the mask I chiefly hate, the malignant thing that has plagued and frightened man since time began. . . ." I hear Donna Durgin, the wife who deserts her family to clerk at Lord & Taylor's, tell Detective Joe Hennessy, "You wouldn't understand. I was dead." "What about your kids? You haven't even asked about them." "What good was I to them? I was disappearing more each day. Is that what life is supposed to be?" I hear Rose Leary defend her Thanksgiving turkey, though her brothers won't eat it, tears glazing her eyes, "Oh, you're all so mean! . . . You know perfectly well there's nothing wrong with that turkey. You just don't want me to stop cooking for you and taking care of this house, you don't want Julian to fall in love with me." I hear Franklin Swift tell us about his lover Zora's visit to his family for Thanksgiving dinner, "Just then my Moms threw her fork down on the table, jumped up, and said, 'Why don't you just shut up!' She dug her fingers in her plate and threw some mashed potatoes in Zora's face." I hear Teddy, my Siamese twin, ask as his brother Leo downs a beer after eighty-nine days off the bottle, "How's that?" and Leo whisper, "Instant hope. I feel *good*!" Lifting cells prick open, the soft punch of happiness, a brightening heavy soak of beautiful feelings . . . "This really is eternal life." I hear Hamlet ask Yorick's skull, "Where be your gibes now? your gambols? your songs? your flashes of merriment that were wont to set the table on a roar? Not one now to mock your own grinning? Quite chop-fallen? Now get you to my lady's chamber, and tell her, let her paint an inch thick, to this favor she must come. Make her laugh at that." I hear Darcy answer Sir William's idea of dancing as "one of the first refinements of polished societies." "Certainly, sir; and it has the advantage also of being in vogue amongst the less polished societies of the world. Every savage can dance." I see distant lightning in black thunderheads, as if repairs are under way at some flawed place in the iron dark of the world, and hear Jimmy Blevins say, I caint be out in this, and Lacey Rawlins tell John Grady, Well. If there was any doubt before I guess that ought to clear it up, and John Grady tell Blevins, You cant outride a thunderstorm. What the hell is wrong with you? I hear Mr. Wilcox admit, "Miss Schlegel, I have had you up on false pretenses. I want to speak about a much more serious matter than a house." "I know—" "Could you be induced to share my—is it probable—" And at "I am asking you to be my wife," Margaret feels an immense joy and all-pervading happiness and the central radiance of love, which later again break over her in waves of emotion as she sits home doing her accounts, amid a tide of passion.

Yes, Forster chooses to swim alone in these feelings and share them with Margaret only secondhand. But even secondhand, Margaret's feelings in the night air prickle our nostrils like the resinous dark smell of a fir just felled for Christmas. Could there be a better life than having these voices rise from our breasts and move others? Than to awaken in our inmost being the word that highlights the eyeball and moves the reader to say, "This makes my heart pine and could not be said better"?

Like storekeepers at the old mom-and-pop grocery, far from the big deal on Broadway or in Hollywood, we sit alone at the Corner Dream Shop in South Bend or Greenwich Village and muse privately on our handcrafted lines and on what Margaret told Henry. No, we don't have inspired actors to help boost our characters' through-lines, or directors to sharpen our pace, or researchers to help dress our sets, or film editors to draw unexpected energies from odd splicings, or cameramen to lend Rembrandt lighting and sculpt shadows and catch the rose glow of our leading lady—hell, we don't even have Technicolor. It's a miracle our readers feel anything without orchestral under-scoring and wind-driven leaves rising in slow motion against the love theme. Like Wild Bill, alone with his muttering murderers or suddenly fixed in a coma hearing Hamlet's grim jests with Yorick's skull, we have only ourselves to draw from.

Play of heart is all. All we need, all we have. All!

Bloomsday, 1993
Greenwich Village

Index